Paul, the Spirit, and the People of God

GORDON D. FEE

HENDRICKSON
PUBLISHERS

© 1996 by Hendrickson Publishers, Inc.
P. O. Box 3473
Peabody, Massachusetts 01961-3473
All rights reserved
Printed in the United States of America

ISBN 1-56563-170-6

Fifth Printing — March 2003

Portions of this book are adapted from *God's Empowering Presence: The Holy Spirit in the Letters of Paul,* © 1994 by Hendrickson Publishers, Inc., Peabody Massachusetts.

Library of Congress Cataloging-in-Publication Data

Fee, Gordon D.
    Paul, the Spirit, and the People of God / Gordon D. Fee.
    Includes bibliographical references and index.
    ISBN 1-56563-170-6
    1. Holy Spirit—Biblical teaching. 2. Bible. N.T. Epistles
of Paul—Theology. 1. Title
BS2655.H67F45   1995
231´.3´0-9015—dc20   95–30872
                                                       CIP

for Maudine—
God's gift of presence in my life,
in our fortieth year

TABLE OF CONTENTS

PREFACE

This book has had a checkered history. It is the book I had hoped to write some years ago at the invitation of Hendrickson Publishers, when they approached me to "expand slightly" the article on the Holy Spirit in the Pauline letters that appeared in the *Dictionary of Pentecostal and Charismatic Movements* (Grand Rapids: Zondervan, 1988). To my great surprise I discovered while writing this article that there was no book available on this subject. So I set out to write a book that would fill this gap.

But I was also anxious to support the conclusions set forth in the dictionary article. So I decided that I needed to give full and careful exegesis to every Pauline text that mentioned the Spirit or the Spirit's activity. The result, *God's Empowering Presence* (Peabody, Mass.: Hendrickson, 1994; henceforth *GEP*), was a massive tome, full of (necessary) detail and careful argumentation.

Thus the first go around resulted in a book targeted primarily for scholars and pastors, and attempted to bring some balance in our presentations of Pauline theology. Even though broad lip service has been paid to the Spirit's rather significant role in Pauline life and thought, New Testament scholarship in general and Pauline scholars in particular have greatly marginalized that role. I wrote *GEP* in part to address that situation.

What led to this presentation of the material has been my fear that Paul's own urgencies—as I perceive them—might have been buried under either the sheer weight of the first book or the catalogue-like presentation of the theology in the final four chapters.

This book attempts to make that material more accessible to a wider audience. It is not simply the "big book" reprinted without the over seven hundred pages of exegesis. Rather, even though most of the content that appears here is from *GEP*, I have largely rewritten and reordered it so that my own urgencies are more clearly in focus. For the exegetical basis of much that appears here, the reader is regularly referred to the appropriate pages of *GEP*.

All of this has been helped along the way by three people. First, Patrick Alexander of Hendrickson Publishers, who edited the first book, has persistently encouraged me to take the time to write this one. Second, Chris Armstrong was asked by Hendrickson to do an initial rewrite of chapters 1 and 12–16 of *GEP* in order to make the material more reader friendly. His suggestive rewriting has served as the basis for much of this book. Third, Wendy Zoba of *Christianity Today* pursued the possibility of my condensing the conclusions of *GEP* into a magazine-length article. In attempting to do so, I finally came to terms with my urgencies and priorities for the present volume.

To give the reader an idea as to what drives this book, I here spell out those urgencies (slightly modified from the form I first presented to Wendy):

a. The bottom line is something that is probably picked up only at the end of *GEP*, namely, the generally ineffective witness and perceived irrelevancy of the church in Western culture. Here, it seems to me, is where the real difference between Paul and us emerges, where in a culture similar to ours the early believers seem to have been more effective than we are. I am convinced this is due in large part to their experience of the reality of the Spirit's presence.

b. This is the concern, then, that makes me uncomfortable with the sometimes either/or approach to the Spirit (between "gifts" and "fruit") that appears to mark much of contemporary Christianity. The Spirit was an empowering presence for the early church, and power had to do with fruit, witness, and gifts.

c. Crucial to this experience was the early church's understanding of the Spirit as the fulfillment of Jewish hopes of the return of the divine presence (hence the utter importance of the temple imagery in Paul). What this meant for early Christians was that the Spirit was not only the personal presence of God in and among them (both individually and corporately) but that their understanding of God had to be broadened so as to become trinitarian. Although he did not use this kind of language, Paul's new understanding of existence (as being in Christ) was thus fully trinitarian at its core.

d. Equally crucial to the experience of the Spirit was the early church's self-understanding as "thoroughly eschatological," in the "already/not yet" sense. The first believers really believed that the future had begun, being attested by the gift of the outpoured Spirit, who also served as the guarantee of the future consummation.

e. At the heart of this new understanding was their perception of themselves as the newly constituted people of God. The goal of salvation in Christ, the core of Pauline theology, was that God should create "a people for his name." And the gift of the eschatological Spirit (the Spirit who served as the evidence that the future had come and the guarantee of its consummation) lies at the heart of such salvation. Central to their new understanding was that one now entered the people of God individually—through faith in Christ and especially through the experienced reality of the Spirit.

f. Although persons individually became members of the people of God, the goal was not simply to fit individuals for heaven but to create a people who by the power of the Spirit lived out the life of the future (the life of God himself) in the present age. The "fruit of the Spirit," therefore, while effected through individual participation, has primarily to do with the life of the community—as does Paul's ethics in general.

g. The "doxological Spirit," who is now the key player in the worship of the newly constituted people of God, also gifts the people so that both in their gifting as such and in the diversity of that gifting, the whole body will be built up to live its new eschatological existence while believers await the final coming of God.

This personal, powerful, experience of the eschatological Spirit not only transformed them individually but made them effective in their being the people of the good news in pagan Greco-Roman culture. And this is why I think they had the better of it, and why we would do well to recapture something of that reality.

This earlier communication of my concerns has served as the basic outline for what follows.

I need to thank four others who read the entire manuscript and offered many helpful suggestions to improve the content and to make it more reader friendly: my present teaching assistant, Dean Pinter, who also created the Scripture index; my daughter—and present student at Regent College—Cherith

Nordling; my son Mark, who read it through the eyes of a pastor for the sake of his people; and especially my wife, Maudine, who patiently worked through the whole to remove some of the "fat" and the "professorial talk," and whose own turns of phrase I borrowed from time to time. I gladly dedicate it to her, my wonderful friend and companion, in this our fortieth anniversary year.

A few further notations about unusual usages, derived from my work on *GEP*, should also help the reader.

First, despite some (expected) objections, I continue to base my theology of Paul on all thirteen of the canonical letters attributed to him. Those who have objected have yet to do so in a way that convinces me to do otherwise.

Second, most lists of references follow what I perceive as the chronological order of these letters: 1 and 2 Thessalonians, 1 and 2 Corinthians, Galatians, Romans, Philemon, Colossians, Ephesians, Philippians, 1 Timothy, Titus, 2 Timothy.

Third, translations that are not noted (NIV, NRSV, etc.) are my own, although at times I have only slightly altered existing translations.

Fourth, in chapter 2 of *GEP* I offered a somewhat technical overview of all uses of *pneuma* ("Spirit/spirit") and *pneumatikos* ("spiritual") in the Pauline corpus. Two conclusions that affect translation and usage are noted here for the sake of the present reader.

a. In some places it is extremely difficult to distinguish between Paul's own "spirit" and the role of the Holy Spirit. For example, when he says in 1 Corinthians 14:15, "my *pneuma* prays," the context makes it certain that Paul intends something like, "the Holy Spirit prays through my own spirit." I have translated such usages with the inelegant "S/spirit," in order to preserve the ambiguity as well as to point to the role of the Spirit in such passages.

b. The evidence is overwhelming that Paul, quite in keeping with first-century usage, never intended *pneumatikos* to refer either to the human spirit or to some vague idea like "spiritual," which in English serves as an adjective meaning "religious," "nonmaterial," "spooky," "nonsecular," or "godly." In every instance in Paul its primary referent is to the Holy Spirit, even when contrasted with "material blessings" in 1 Corinthians 9:11. Thus I regularly capitalize this adjective (Spiritual; cf. Spirituality) when I use it in the Pauline way; "spiritual" occurs when it is used in a more contemporary way.

Fifth, one of the shortcomings of this book is that I have not tried to compare Paul with the other writers of the New Testament. My aim has been to hear Paul on his own terms. Hopefully, it will stand alongside other books of its kind: by Gary Burge (for John); James Shelton (for Luke–Acts); and Gerald Hawthorne (for Jesus).

Finally, the writing of GEP has transformed my own life. I have been gratified—and humbled—to learn from a goodly number of others, by letter, phone, or personal conversation, that reading the exegetical portions of that book has enriched them. I offer the present version of this material with the fervent prayer that it may have a similar effect on many who read it.

Epiphany 1996

OVERTURE—
AN INVITATION TO
READ PAUL ANEW

*One reads Paul poorly who does not recognize
that for him the presence of the Spirit, as an
experienced and living reality, was the crucial
matter for Christian life, from beginning to end.*

Contemporary Christians have a right to be concerned. In an increasingly secular, individualistic, and relativistic world—dubbed
"post-Christian" in the 1960s and now called "postmodern"—the
church is regularly viewed as irrelevant at best and Neanderthal at
worst. Frankly, much of the fault lies with the church, especially
those of us in the church who pride ourselves in being orthodox
with regard to the historic faith. For all too often our orthodoxy
has been either diluted by an unholy alliance with a given political
agenda, or diminished by legalistic or relativistic ethics quite unrelated to the character of God, or rendered ineffective by a pervasive
rationalism in an increasingly nonrationalistic world.

But there is reason for hope as well since contemporary postmodernism looks much like the culture of the Greco-Roman world
into which the gospel first appeared some two thousand years ago.
The secret to the success of the early believers in their culture lay
first with their "good news" centered in the life, death, and resurrection of Jesus. Immanuel had come, bringing both revelation of
the character of God ("Have you been with me for so long and

don't know who I am? The one who has seen me has seen the Father," John 14:9) and redemption from our tragic fallenness ("You shall call his name Yeshua, for he will save his people from their sins," Matt 1:21). But their success also lay with their experienced life of the Spirit who made the work of Christ an effective reality in their lives, thus making them a radical alternative within their culture.

It often seems otherwise with us. If we have (rightly) kept our central focus on Christ Jesus, we are less sure about the Holy Spirit. Despite the affirmations in our creeds and hymns and the lip service paid to the Spirit in our occasional conversations, the Spirit has been largely marginalized both in the halls of learning and in the life of the church as a community of faith.

I do not mean that the Holy Spirit is not present; he is indeed, or we are not of Christ at all. But the primary emphasis regarding the Spirit's activity has been on his quiescence, based largely on imagery drawn from Elijah's encounter with God on Sinai, where the Lord was not in the wind, earthquake, and fire, but came to Elijah "in a still small voice" (1 Kgs 19:11–13 KJV). Support for this view is then found in the New Testament by emphasizing Paul's "fruit of the Spirit" (Gal 5:22–23), while suggesting that the "gifts of the Spirit" in 1 Corinthians 12–14 were for the apostolic period only. Quiescence, however, has sometimes fostered anemia, not only in the church corporately but also at the individual level, evidenced in part by the myriad of ways individual believers have longed for a greater sense of God's presence in their lives.

This common "missing out" on the Spirit as an experienced, empowering reality has frequently been "corrected" historically through a variety of Spirit movements—most recently in this century in the form of the Pentecostal and charismatic movements. Emphasis here has been on the "wind, earthquake, and fire," and the primary texts are from Acts and 1 Corinthians 12–14. These Spirit movements have also tended to emphasize individualistic spirituality, so that the reality of the Spirit is sometimes merely experienced in the experience. Such piety has frequently lacked sound exegetical basis or betrayed inadequate theological reflection.

The net result has tended toward a truncated view of the Spirit on both sides, accompanied by an inadequate view of the role of the Spirit in Paul's understanding of things Christian. For him life in the Spirit meant embracing both fruit and gifts simultaneously and vigorously—what I have come to call life in the radical middle. The Spirit as an experienced and empowering reality was for Paul and his churches the key player in all of Christian life, from beginning to end. The Spirit covered the whole waterfront: power for life, growth, fruit, gifts, prayer, witness, and everything else.

But if the empowering, experienced dimension of life in the Spirit is often missed on the one side, too often missing on both sides are two further matters that, for Paul, lie at the very heart of faith. First, the Spirit as person, the promised return of God's own personal presence with his people; second, the Spirit as eschatological fulfillment (see ch. 5 below), who both reconstitutes God's people anew and empowers us to live the life of the future in our between-the-times existence—between the time of Christ's first and second coming.

If the church is going to be effective in our postmodern world, we need to stop paying mere lip service to the Spirit and to recapture Paul's perspective: the Spirit as the *experienced, empowering* return of God's own *personal presence* in and among us, who enables us to live as a radically *eschatological* people in the present world while we await the consummation. All the rest, including fruit and gifts (that is, ethical life and charismatic utterances in worship), serve to that end.

Hence I offer this "invitation" to read Paul afresh, to recognize the crucial role of the Spirit in his life and thought, and in that of his churches. Such a reading, I insist, must be thoroughly exegetical—hence the frequent references to the exegesis presented in GEP— and fully theological, to see how the Spirit fits into the bigger picture of things Pauline. This fresh reading of Paul will make clear that for him the presence of the Spirit, as an experienced and living reality, was the crucial matter for Christian life, from beginning to end. Since that is a theological assertion, some preliminary theological issues must first be addressed in chapter 1. I encourage readers not to get bogged down here. The chapter is necessary in order to establish a reference point for the rest of the book.

A "THEOLOGY" OF THE SPIRIT? THE SPIRIT IN PAULINE THEOLOGY

Our theology and experience of the Spirit must
be more interwoven if our experienced life
of the Spirit is to be more effective.

I well remember my graduate theology professor declaring emphatically: "*Everyone* has a theology [that is, some rudimentary view of God and the world on the basis of which they live]; the question is not *whether* you have a theology—you do—but whether you have a *good* one."

Without apology, therefore, this is primarily a book on Paul's *theology*, that is, how Paul understood God and his ways, and the role of the Spirit in that theology. For some, of course, a "theology" book on the Spirit is the kiss of death; and in many ways I am in that camp. But we lack a better word; and in the final analysis, the health of the contemporary church necessitates that its *theology* of the Spirit and its *experience* of the Spirit correspond much more closely than they have in much of the past.

Ordinarily theology has to do with a studied, reflective understanding of things divine, dealing with how the various matters we believe about God and God's ways can be put into a coherent whole. But we do not find Paul reflecting on the Holy Spirit, any more than we find him reflecting on the significance of the Lord's Table or on the relationships within the Godhead, which he presupposes and which tantalizingly pop out here and there. As often happens with such foundational matters, we rarely look at them reflectively. They are simply part of the stuff of ongoing life; and what we say about them is often offhanded, matter-of-fact, and without argument or explanation.

Yet theology is what Paul is doing all the time. Rather than the reflective theology of the scholar or classroom, his is a "task theology," the theologizing that takes place in the marketplace, where belief and the experience of God run head-on into the thought systems, religions, and everyday life of people in the Greco-Roman world at the beginning of the second half of the first century. Paul's task theology is the more complex because it takes place in a racially and socially diverse environment. In part, therefore, the issues raised for Paul have to do with what the God of the Jews (the one and only God) was doing in history through Christ and the Spirit, which for Paul transpired within a primarily Gentile context.

Into this kind of setting Paul came preaching, experiencing, rethinking, and restating old and new truths, as he wrestled with what it meant for Jew and Gentile together to be the one people of God. In the process he was constantly "doing" theology, grappling with how the gospel works—and works out—in this new context that was so radically different from the more insular Jewish world in which the gospel first appeared in history.

Our present concern in this reading of Paul is with what he *says* about the Spirit, since his words are our primary window into his understanding. But we need to do more than just gather all the passages and test them against some set of doctrinal assumptions, for in the case of the Spirit we are dealing with the essential matter of early Christian *experience*. The only worthwhile theology, after all, is one that is translated into life; and Paul's understanding of the Spirit is ultimately a matter of lived-out faith. The experience of the Spirit was how the early believers came to receive the salvation that Christ had brought, and how they came to understand themselves as living at the beginning of the end times. For them, the Spirit was both the evidence that God's great future for his people had already made its way into the present and the guarantee that God would conclude what he had begun in Christ

(= Paul's eschatological framework). Thus the Spirit is foundational to their entire *experience* and *understanding* of their present life in Christ.

My concern is that we come to terms both with the experienced realities and with Paul's understanding of them, as much as we can do that fairly and with integrity.

CONTINUITY AND DISCONTINUITY WITH THE PAST

One of the primary issues in Pauline theology is that of continuity and discontinuity between the old covenant and the new—that is, between God's word to Israel, communicated by prophet and poet, and God's new word to his people through Christ Jesus, communicated by apostles and teachers. We read the letters of Paul as part of the New Testament, the record of God's new covenant with his people, effected through Christ and the Spirit. But in fact Paul did not know he was contributing to such a "new testament." For him the "new covenant" was not a written record at all but a historical reality, experienced anew at the Table of the Lord and realized on an everyday basis through the presence of the Spirit. The question then is, How is the new related to the old? Does it *supersede,* as a truly *new* covenant? Or does it *fulfill,* and in so doing carry with it much of what was there before? In order to understand Paul properly we must grasp how his perspective both continues and modifies the religious tradition in which he was reared, especially his understanding of his Old Testament roots.

One of the primary issues in Pauline theology is that of continuity and discontinuity between the old covenant and the new.

First, we must recognize his own sense of continuity with his heritage. Paul sees himself and his churches as being in a direct line with the people of God in the Old Testament; and despite his deep convictions about the radical implications of the coming of Christ and the Spirit, he regularly reaffirms that continuity. He includes a primarily Gentile church in the events of the exodus: "all *our* forefathers were baptized into Moses in the cloud and in the sea" (1 Cor 10:1–2). To Gentiles who were in danger of submitting to circumcision he not only appeals to Abraham and the promises of the old covenant, but also asks frankly, "Tell me, you who wish to be under the law, do you not hear the law?" and then expounds the "true meaning" of Sarah and Hagar, Isaac and Ishmael, in light of Christ and the Spirit (Gal 4:21–31). Paul never speaks of a "new Israel" or "new people of God"; his language is "God's Israel" (Gal 6:16), an *Israel* in continuation with the past but now composed of Jew and Gentile alike as the one people of God.

But just as clearly, there is significant discontinuity. The people of God have now been newly formed. Christ is the "goal of the law" (Rom 10:4), and the Spirit is "the promised Holy Spirit" (Gal 3:14; Eph 1:13). Christ's death and resurrection have brought an end to Torah observance (living on the basis of the Old Testament law, Rom 7:4–6; 8:2–3); being led by the Spirit has replaced observance as God's way of fulfilling Torah (Gal 5:18); indeed, the righteous requirement of Torah is now fulfilled in those who walk in/by the Spirit (Rom 8:4).

The Holy Spirit was an essential part of Israel's promised future. For Paul the gift of "the Holy Spirit of promise" (Eph 1:13) is the certain evidence that the future has already been set in motion. To see how the promise has been fulfilled by the Spirit, and how that affected the early church's self-understanding, is part of the invitation to this fresh reading of Paul.

Since the Spirit plays this integral role in fulfilling the promised new covenant, it would be fitting to include a chapter in this book on the Pauline antecedents,[1] that is, on the role of the Spirit in the Old Testament and intertestamental Judaism. Rather than do that, I have chosen to show throughout the book what their expectations looked like and how Paul understands the Spirit as fulfilling them.

FINDING THE ELUSIVE CENTER

A final introductory word concerns the long debate in scholarship as to what constitutes the "heart" of Paul's theology.[2] The traditional view, fostered by the Reformers and perpetuated by generations of Protestants, is that "justification by faith" is the key to that theology. This view emphasizes Christ's historical saving act on our behalf and our realization of it through faith. The inadequacy of this view is that it focuses on one metaphor of salvation, justification, to the exclusion of others.[3] Such a focus fails to throw the net broadly enough to capture all of Paul's theological concerns.

In response to this, others found as the center Paul's "mystical experience of being *in Christ*."[4] This view shifted the focus from Christ's historical work and its appropriation by the believer to the believer's (especially Paul's) ongoing experience of Christ. While in some ways this view served as a corrective to the traditional one, most contemporary Pauline scholars have recognized that both these approaches are somewhat limiting. The frequent result, however, has been to emphasize the diversity and "contingency"[5] of Paul's letters to such an extent that many scholars, reflecting contemporary postmodernism, despair of ever finding a genuine center to Pauline theology—or even of finding coherence in his theology at all.

I bring two convictions to these matters regarding Pauline theology. First, I am convinced that there is a stable core to Paul's understanding of Christ and the Spirit, much of which he presupposes, based on his sense of continuity with the old, and all of which can be found in what he simply calls "the gospel." For him there was a fundamental core content to the gospel—a content held in common with all other early Christians (see, e.g., 1 Cor 15:1–3, 11). The seeming variations in Paul's theology, as I understand them, have to do with his working through the implications of that common content for the Gentile mission, to which he devoted the last two decades of his life.

Second, and in keeping with some of the present mood, I am convinced that the center is so elusive because the basic core of

Paul's theology covers too much ground for one to simplify it into a single phrase. It would seem far better for us to isolate the essential elements of his theology that lie at the heart of matters for Paul and around which all other concerns cluster. In my view, at least four elements are essential:

— The *church* as an eschatological community (that is, a community living in the "beginning of the end times") made up of the new covenant people of God.

— The *eschatological framework* of this new people's existence and thinking.

— The formation of God's new people by the eschatological *salvation* accomplished through the *death and resurrection of Christ.*

— The focus of this people on *Jesus* as Messiah, Lord, and Son of God.

To put this another way:

— The *foundation:* A gracious and merciful God, who is full of love toward all.

— The *framework:* The fulfillment of God's promises as already begun but not yet completed.

— The *focus:* Jesus, the Son of God, who as God's suffering servant Messiah accomplished eschatological salvation for humanity through his death and resurrection, and who is now the exalted Lord and coming King.

— The *fruit:* The church as an eschatological community, who, formed as a people by Christ's death and the gift of the Spirit, and thus restored into God's likeness, becomes God's new covenant people.

If this is a correct assessment of Paul's perspective (and indeed that of the rest of the New Testament), then we might further distill all of this. On the one hand, as will be pointed out in chapter 5, it seems impossible to understand Paul without recognizing *eschatology* as the essential framework of all his theological thinking; on the other hand, *salvation in Christ* is the essential concern within that framework. Salvation is "eschatological" in the sense that final salvation, which still awaits the believer, is already a present reality through Christ and the Spirit. It is "in Christ" in the sense that what originated in God was effected historically by the death and resurrection of Christ, and is received and experienced by God's people through the work of the Holy Spirit—who is also the key to Christian life "between the times," until the final consummation at Christ's parousia ("coming").

It is fair to say that "Paul's entire theology without the supporting pinion of the Spirit would crumble into ruins."

It does not take much reflection to recognize that apart from the actual focus on Jesus Christ as Messiah, Lord, and Savior, the Spirit is a crucial ingredient to each of these aspects of the Pauline center. Thus my conviction that the Spirit stands near the center of things for Paul, as part of the fundamental core of his understanding of the gospel. The experience of the Spirit is the key to his already/not yet eschatological framework; the Spirit is the essential player in the believers' experiencing and living out the salvation that God has brought about in Christ; the Spirit both forms the church into God's new (eschatological) people and conforms them into Christ's image through his fruit in their lives; and the Spirit gifts them in worship to edify and encourage one another in their ongoing life in the world. It is fair to say that "Paul's entire theology without the supporting pinion of the Spirit would crumble into ruins."[6]

Finally, I must note that the aim of all this is not simply informational. I would be less than honest if I did not admit to trying to persuade. But persuasion in this case is not a matter of being right or wrong. My ultimate concern, for myself and for the contemporary church, is that we return to our biblical roots on this matter if the church is going to count for anything in the new millennium that lies just around the corner.

NOTES

1. Which is precisely what I did as an appendix in *GEP*, 904–15.

2. For a helpful overview of this debate, especially in its more recent expressions, see J. Plevnik, "The Center of Pauline Theology," *Catholic Biblical Quarterly* 61 (1989) 461–78.

3. "Justification" is a term drawn from the law courts. It is a natural metaphor to use when the Jewish law is in purview; indeed, it is used almost exclusively in such settings. Elsewhere Paul uses a variety of metaphors, drawn from a variety of social settings: for example, redemption (in the context of slavery), adoption (a family metaphor; see ch. 6 below), propitiation (taken from the sacrificial system), washing (also from Jewish religious practices), reconciliation (in the context of enmity between persons).

4. See *GEP*, 12, n. 13.

5. At issue for many is the relationship of coherence and contingency in trying to reconstruct Pauline theology. That is, can one extrapolate a coherent theological core from Paul's letters to serve as a kind of Pauline "systematic" theology? Or does the ad hoc nature of the letters, which means that the theology is always being expressed in the contingency of that historically specific situation, preclude finding such coherence?

6. C. Pinnock, "The Concept of Spirit in the Epistles of Paul" (Ph.D. dissertation; Manchester, 1963) 2; cf. S. Neill and N. T. Wright, *The Interpretation of the New Testament 1861–1986* (Oxford: Oxford University Press, 1988) 203: "Paul's doctrine of the Spirit is far more central and characteristic than his doctrine of justification by faith."

GOD REVISITS HIS PEOPLE—THE SPIRIT AS THE RENEWED PRESENCE OF GOD

*The outpouring of the Spirit meant for Paul
that God had fulfilled his promise to dwell
once again in and among his people.*

Presence is a delicious word—because it points to one of our truly great gifts. Nothing else can take the place of presence, not gifts, not telephone calls, not pictures, not mementos, nothing. Ask the person who has lost a lifelong mate what they miss the most; the answer is invariably "presence." When we are ill, we don't need soothing words nearly as much as we need loved ones to be present. What makes shared life—games, walks, concerts, outings, and a myriad of other things—so pleasurable? Presence.

God has made us this way, in his own image, because he himself is a personal, relational being. The great problem with the fall is that we lost not only our vision of God (that is, his true character has been distorted) but also our relationship with God, and thus no longer knew his abiding presence. For Paul the coming of Christ and the Spirit changed all of this forever.

At the heart of things Pauline is his understanding of the outpoured Spirit as the coming of "the promised Holy Spirit" (Eph 1:13; Gal 3:14). While this promise especially included the renewal of the prophetic word,[1] for Paul it also meant the arrival of the new covenant, anticipated by the promised "circumcision of the heart" in Deuteronomy 30:6 and prophesied explicitly in Jeremiah 31:31–34: "I will make a new covenant . . . and I will write it on their hearts" (NRSV). This prophecy was shortly thereafter picked up by Ezekiel, who expressly linked it to the Spirit, whom God was going to "put in you" (36:26–27; 37:14). Above everything else, as fulfillment of the new covenant[2] the Spirit marked the return of the lost presence of God.

Here, then, is one of the more significant areas where the Spirit represents both continuity and discontinuity between the old and new covenants. The continuity is to be found in the promised renewal of God's presence with his people; the discontinuity lies in the radically new way God has revisited them—indwelling them individually as well as corporately by his Spirit.

THE PRESENCE OF GOD IN THE OLD TESTAMENT

The theme of the presence of God is crucial to both the Old and New Testaments, serving in fact as bookends to the Christian Bible.[3] It begins in Genesis 2–3 with the creator of heaven and earth being present in the garden with those he has created in his own image; it concludes with the marvelous pictures of the renewed heaven and earth and the renewal of Eden in Revelation 21:1–22:5, in which John says expressly, "I saw no temple in the city, for its temple is the Lord God Almighty and the Lamb" (21:22 NRSV). Whatever else, the people of Israel understood themselves to be the people of the Presence, the people among whom the eternal God had chosen to dwell on earth.

The Tabernacle and Temple

The most prominent way God's presence is experienced in the Old Testament is in the tabernacle and the temple. Such a presence motif, culminating in God's glory descending on the tabernacle, is the structural key to the book of Exodus. In the incident of the burning bush (Exod 3), the living God first shows himself present to Moses at Sinai. Then he instructs Moses to bring the people there to worship him. When Israel arrives at the holy mount in ch. 19, they come to the place of God's "dwelling," the place they are forbidden even to touch on penalty of death. Only Moses is allowed into God's presence.

But God plans to move from the mount and dwell among his people by means of a tabernacle. So after the giving of the Book of the Covenant (Exod 20-24), Moses receives the instructions for the tabernacle's construction (chs. 25-31). But between the instructions and the construction (chs. 35-39), the disastrous episode in the desert occurs (ch. 32), followed by God's announcing to Moses: "My presence will not go with you"; an angel will go instead (ch. 33). Moses recognizes the inadequacy of this solution and intercedes: "If your Presence does not go with us, do not send us up from here. How will anyone know that you are pleased with me and with your people unless you go with us? What else will distinguish me and your people from all the other people on the face of the earth?" (33:15-16 NIV).

This is followed by the further revelation of God's character ("compassionate, gracious, slow to anger, abounding in love and faithfulness," Exod 34:4-7) and the construction of the tabernacle, all of which concludes with the descent of God's glory, which "filled the tabernacle" (40:35). With that, they are ready to journey to the place that "the Lord your God will choose as a dwelling for his name" (Deut 12:11 and passim), led by the presence of God symbolized by the pillar of cloud and the pillar of fire.

The Deuteronomy promise was finally fulfilled in the construction of Solomon's temple, where the same glory as in Exodus 40 descended and "filled his temple" (1 Kgs 8:11). Thus Jerusalem and the temple are regularly described as "the place Yahweh chose for his name to dwell"; and the temple became the focal point of Israel's existence in the promised land.

More even than the law, therefore, or other identity markers such as circumcision, food laws, and Sabbath observance, God's presence with Israel distinguished them as his people. They well understood that the God who created the heavens and the earth could not be contained by an earthly structure (e.g., Isa 66:1–2); nonetheless, because God chose to have his presence concentrate there, the tabernacle and the temple became the primary symbols of God's presence among his people.

Thus, even though the temple also served as a place for sacrifices, the Old Testament people of God saw it primarily as a place of prayer and of knowing God's presence was with them. This comes out over and over again in Israel's hymn book, the Psalter. Take, for example, the great enthronement hymn in Psalm 68, which pictures God's presence on Zion as the hope of his people and the envy of their neighbors:

> The mountains of Bashan are majestic mountains;
>   rugged are the mountains of Bashan.
> Why gaze in envy, O rugged mountains,
>   at the mountain where God chooses to reign
>   where the Lord himself will dwell forever. (Ps 68:15–16)

Of the "enthronement," the psalmist sings:

> The chariots of God are tens of thousands,
>   and thousands of thousands;
> The Lord has come from Sinai into his sanctuary;
> When you ascended on high,
>   you led captives in your train;
>   you received gifts from people
> even from the rebellious—
>   that you, O Lord, might dwell there. (vv. 17–18 NIV)

This same theme is repeatedly picked up by individual Israelites throughout the Psalter, as they reflect on the glory of being in God's presence:

> How lovely is your dwelling place, O Lord Almighty,
> My soul yearns, even faints, for the courts of the Lord;
>   my heart and my flesh cry out for the living God. (Ps 84:1–2)

> I have seen you in the sanctuary
>   and beheld your power and your glory. (Ps 63:2)

But Israel's failure caused them to forfeit God's presence. This is what makes the fall of Jerusalem and the exile so full of pathos for them. The temple in Jerusalem, where God had chosen to dwell, was destroyed; and not only were the people carried away captive, but the captives and those who remained were no longer a people distinguished by the presence of the living God in their midst. The poignancy of it all finds its ultimate, symbolic expression in Ezekiel 10, where, just as with the ark of the covenant in 1 Samuel 4, the "glory of the Lord" departs from the temple in Jerusalem.

The Promise of the Renewed Presence

But all was not lost. Central to the prophetic hope was the promised return of God's presence. Through Ezekiel, for example, God promises, "My dwelling place will be with them; I will be their God and they will be my people" (37:27); and Malachi prophesies, "Then suddenly the Lord you are seeking will come to his temple" (3:1). This hope continues into intertestamental Judaism among the apocalyptic writers, as, for example, in the *Testament of Dan* 5:13: "And Jerusalem will no longer undergo desolation, . . . because the Lord will be in her midst."

> *Central to the prophetic hope was the promised return of God's presence.*

In keeping with Israel's earlier history, the motif of the renewed presence is tied directly to the hope of a restored temple. The motif finds its most powerful metaphorical expression in Ezekiel's grand vision (chs. 40–48) but its most memorable moment in the oracle of Isaiah 2:2–3 (repeated in Mic 4:1–2), where the inclusion of the Gentiles is also a primary motif[4] (cf. Zech 14:16–19):

In the last days
   the mountain of the Lord's temple will be established
     as chief among the mountains;
it will be raised above the hills,
   and all nations will stream to it.
Many peoples will come and say,
"Come, let us go up to the mountain of the Lord,
   to the house of the God of Jacob.
He will teach us his ways,
   so that we may walk in his paths."

The second temple, however, does not live up to all these expectations. Thus it evinces mixed feelings among the people. In light of Solomon's temple and the promised future temple of Ezekiel, Haggai complains, "Who of you is left who saw this house in its former glory? How does it look to you now? Does it not seem to you like nothing?" (2:3). In many circles, therefore, the hope of a rebuilt, grand temple still awaited the people of God.[5]

The Presence Equated with the Spirit

For Paul the most crucial matter regarding this motif lies with the fact that in Isaiah 63:9–14 the divine presence in the Exodus narrative was specifically equated with "the Holy Spirit of the Lord." In recalling Israel's past, the prophet says:

He became their savior in all their distress.
It was no messenger or angel
  but his Presence that saved them.
In his love and mercy he redeemed them;
  he lifted them up and carried them
  all the days of old.
Yet they rebelled
  and *grieved his Holy Spirit.*
Therefore he became their enemy;
  he himself fought against them.
Then they recalled the days of old,
  of Moses and his people.
Where is he who brought them through the sea,
  with the shepherds of his flock?
Where is he *who set his Holy Spirit among them,*
who sent his glorious arm of power
  to be at Moses' right hand,
who divided the waters before them,
  to make for himself an everlasting name,
  who led them through the depths?
Like a horse in the desert,
  they did not stumble;
like cattle that go down to the plain,
  the Spirit of Yahweh gave them rest.
This is how you guided your people
  to make for yourself a glorious name.[6]

This connection is one with which Paul is thoroughly familiar, as is confirmed by his deliberate echo of the language of v. 10 in Ephesians 4:30: "And do not *grieve the Holy Spirit of God,* with whom you were sealed for the day of redemption."

THE SPIRIT AS THE RENEWED PRESENCE IN PAUL

When we turn to Paul from these (especially) Old Testament antecedents, it is clear that he understands the Spirit's coming as fulfilling three related expectations: (1) the association of the Spirit with the new covenant; (2) the language of "indwelling"; and (3) the association of the Spirit with the imagery of the temple. By fulfilling both the new covenant and the renewed temple motifs, the Spirit becomes the way God himself is now present on planet earth.[7]

For Paul the Spirit is how God presently dwells in his holy temple.

The temple imagery is especially significant in this regard, since the temple was always understood as the *place* of God's dwelling, the place of his glory. For Paul the Spirit is how God presently dwells in his holy temple. Significantly, such dwelling takes place both in the gathered community, as one might well expect given the Old Testament background to this usage, and especially in the heart of the individual believer.

The Spirit's Role in the New Covenant

In keeping with the rest of the early church, Paul recognizes the death of Christ as instituting God's new covenant with his people (see 1 Cor 11:25). He also sees the Spirit as the way that covenant is realized in and among them. As the result of his own—and others'—experience of the Spirit, Paul understands this role especially in terms of Ezekiel 36:26–27 and 37:14. Paul combines motifs from these two passages in such a way that in the coming of the Spirit into the life of the believer and the believing community God fulfilled three dimensions of the promise:

1. God would give his people a "new heart"—Jeremiah's "heart of flesh" to replace that of stone (Jer 31:31-33)—made possible because he would also give them "a new spirit" (Ezek 36:26). In Paul this theme finds expression in 2 Corinthians 3:1-6, where the Corinthians are understood to be the recipients of the new covenant in that they were "inscribed" by "the Spirit of the living God" on "tablets of human hearts" (v. 3). Paul himself is the minister of this new covenant, which no longer has to do with "letter" but with the Spirit who gives life (vv. 5-6). This same understanding lies behind the similar language in Romans 7:5-6, as well as the "circumcision of the heart by the Spirit" in Romans 2:29, which echoes Deuteronomy 30:6 in terms of fulfillment.

2. This "new spirit" is none other than God's Spirit, who will enable God's people to follow his decrees (Ezek 36:27). As is evident in Romans 8:3-4 and Galatians 5:16-25,[8] the Spirit's fulfillment of this theme is Paul's answer to the question of what happens to righteousness if one does away with observance of the Torah (the Old Testament law).

3. God's Spirit means the presence of God himself, in that by putting "my Spirit in you . . . you will live" (Ezek 37:14). Again, Paul picks up this theme in 2 Corinthians 3:5-6. As the Spirit of the living God, the Spirit provides for God's people the one essential reality about God. "The Spirit," Paul says in the context of the new covenant, "gives life."

Similarly, the language of 1 Thessalonians 4:8 is expressly that of Ezekiel 36-37. Any rejection of holiness on the part of the Thessalonians is a rejection of the God who "gives his Holy Spirit into you."[9] It is the presence of the holy God himself, by his Holy Spirit, whom they reject if they reject Paul's call to holy living. We may conclude that for Paul, Christ has made the new covenant effective for the people of God through his death and resurrection; but the Spirit is the key to the new covenant as a fulfilled reality in the lives of God's people.

The Indwelling Spirit

Intimately related to the divine presence theme and the new covenant passages in the Old Testament are the many texts in Paul that speak of the Spirit as dwelling in or among the people of God. This theme is found first of all in the texts that locate the Spirit within the believer. The Spirit is spoken of as being "in you/us" (1 Thess 4:8; 1 Cor 6:19; 14:24-25; Eph 5:18 [in the imagery of "filling"]). The location of "in you/us" is the "heart" (2 Cor 1:22; 3:3; Gal 4:6; Rom 2:29; 5:5). This in turn becomes the language of "dwelling in" (1 Cor 3:16; 2 Cor 6:16; Rom 8:9-11; Eph 2:22).

It is especially with temple imagery that Paul designates the Spirit as the renewed presence of God among his people.

Two of these passages (1 Cor 14:24-25 and 2 Cor 6:16) are especially instructive in that Paul cites Old Testament texts that speak of God's dwelling in the midst of his people, which Paul now attributes to the presence of the Spirit. When pagans turn to the living God because their hearts have been exposed through the prophetic Spirit, Paul speaks of this in the language of Isaiah 45:14: "Surely God is among you."

Similarly, in the temple imagery of 2 Corinthians 6:16, which presupposes the presence of the Spirit in the life of the community from 1 Corinthians 3:16, Paul understands God to be present among his people. In making that point, he draws on the language of the new covenant promise of Ezekiel 37:27: "I will dwell among them and they shall be my people." This latter passage points toward the ultimate expression of the language of indwelling—in the imagery of the temple.

The Church as God's Temple

It is especially with temple imagery that Paul designates the Spirit as the renewed presence of God among his people. This imagery occurs four times in Paul, three times in keeping with its

Old Testament precedents (1 Cor 3:16–17; 2 Cor 6:16; Eph 2:22), where God dwells in the midst of the people by means of tabernacle and temple, and once in keeping with the promised new covenant (1 Cor 6:19–20), where the "temple" is now the body of the believer, "who is in you, whom you have received from God."

First, then, Paul specifically ties the Spirit to temple imagery in the context of the Spirit's presence in the midst of the people of God. Here is how the living God is now present with his people, expressed most clearly in Ephesians 2:22: the church is being raised up to become a holy temple in the Lord, built up together as "a dwelling for God by his Spirit."

Here lies the significance of 1 Corinthians 3:16–17.[10] Paul's introductory, "do you not know that . . . " followed by "you are the temple of God [in Corinth]," plus the argument in context, make clear that the Spirit as fulfilling the temple/presence of God motif is the rich history that Paul has in mind. In context he is arguing with those who are in the process of destroying the church in Corinth by their contention over leaders in the name of (merely human) wisdom. In response Paul moves from words about the folly of their making "lords" of merely human servants in vv. 5–9, to words of warning in vv. 10–15 toward those currently leading the church in this disastrous direction, and finally to words that address the church itself in terms of who they are as the people of God in Corinth—namely, God's temple in Corinth.

Paul's use of the temple imagery begins in v. 9 ("you [the church in Corinth] are God's building"). Their foundation (Christ crucified) had been laid by the apostle, but at the time of Paul's letter the superstructure was being erected with materials incompatible with that foundation (wood and straw, referring to their current fascination with wisdom and rhetoric). They must build with enduring materials (gold, silver, costly stones = the gospel of the Crucified One), imagery taken from the building of Solomon's temple (1 Chron 29:2; 2 Chron 3:6). Then in v. 16 Paul asks rhetorically, "Do you not know what kind of building you are? God's temple in Corinth!" As a gathered community, they formed the one temple of the living God, God's alternative to Corinth's countless pagan temples; and what made them his alternative was the presence of the Spirit in their midst.

But the Corinthians were in the process of dismantling God's temple, because their strife and fascination with wisdom meant the banishing of the revealing and unifying Spirit from their midst.[11] Hence this strongest of warnings: the people responsible for the destruction would themselves be destroyed by God. He will do this precisely because his temple, the place of his presence, is holy; and "you the church in Corinth are that temple." The gathered church is the place of God's own personal presence, by the Spirit. This is what marks off God's new people from "all the other people on the face of the earth" (Exod 33:16).

There is not a more important word in all the New Testament as to the nature of the local church than this one! The local church is God's temple in the community where it is placed; and it is so by the presence of the Spirit alone, by whom God has now revisited his people. It is no wonder, therefore, that Paul sees the expulsion of the incestuous man from their corporate fellowship (they are not even to eat with him) as ultimately leading to his salvation (1 Cor 5:1–13). Being put outside the place of God's presence will apparently lead to his repentance, so that he may be saved, by being once more among the people of the Presence.

This emphasis on the church as God's temple, and therefore God's alternative to the pagan temples of Corinth, also lies behind the identical imagery in 2 Corinthians 6:16–7:1. Those in the church must come out from the idolatry of Corinth (repeating the prohibition of 1 Cor 8–10) and purify themselves from every defilement, because they are God's temple, the place of the eternal God's dwelling in Corinth.

In urging his readers in Ephesians 4:30 "not to grieve the Holy Spirit of God," Paul uses the language of Isaiah 63:10, the one certain place in the Old Testament where the concept of the divine presence with Israel in tabernacle and temple is specifically equated with "the Holy Spirit of Yahweh." This equation is the basis of Paul's warning. The divine presence in the form of God's own Spirit, not an angel or envoy, journeyed with God's people in the desert. By the Holy Spirit, God's presence has now returned to his people, to indwell them corporately and individually so that they might walk in his ways. Paul therefore urges the Ephesians not to repeat Israel's failure. They are not, through various sins of discord that destroy the "unity of the Spirit" (4:3), to grieve the God who is present among them by his Holy Spirit.

The Individual Believer as God's Temple

In 1 Corinthians 6:19–20, Paul makes the remarkable transfer of this imagery from the church to the individual believer. Thus God not only dwells in the midst of his people by the Spirit, but has likewise taken up residence in the lives of his people individually by the same life-giving Spirit.

The significance of this transfer of images should not be missed. The context has to do with sexual immorality. Paul's concern is with the "sanctification" of the believer. Reflecting an understanding of the time that sharply distinguished between physical, material reality and the immaterial, invisible realm (Hellenistic dualism), some Corinthians were suggesting that the human spirit was not affected by what happens to one's body, including having sex with prostitutes. But Paul will have none of that. The God who created us in his image created the body as well as the spirit, and thus pronounced the material order to be good.

In this final moment of argument with them, Paul appeals to the presence of the Spirit in their lives in the context of the saving work of Christ. In "purchasing" them for God's glory, Christ also purchased their bodies, as evidenced by the Holy Spirit, whose temple they are because God now dwells not in temples made by human hands, but in temples constructed by his own hands. Thus they are not their own, to do with their bodies as they please. They belong to the God who purchased them through Christ's sacrifice and now indwells them by his Spirit.[12]

In this text, as well as in 2 Corinthians 2:14–4:6, lies the secret to Paul's personal piety and to his understanding of the Spirit in his own life. In both cases the texts finally point outward; that is, the goal of this dimension of Spirit life is not simply contemplation but the ethical life that the Spirit produces. Nonetheless, the personal dimension cannot be set aside. Indeed, the first location of God's presence in the new covenant is within his people individually, sanctifying their present existence and stamping it with his eternity.

But as is often true of imagery in Paul, by its flexibility it can take a different turn in another context. Part of our way into a proper understanding of 2 Corinthians 2:14–4:6 is again through the combined imagery of tabernacle/ temple and presence.[13] It begins in 2:17 with Paul's arguing regarding the validity of his ministry—in contrast to the peddlers of another gospel—that he makes his claim as one who "lives in the presence of God."

For Paul, the Spirit is not merely an impersonal force or influence or power. The Spirit is none other than the fulfillment of the promise that God himself would once again be present with his people.

This theme is then picked up in 3:7 and carried through to the end by the contrast of his ministry with that of Moses. This treatment evolves eventually into a kind of midrash (that is, a traditional Jewish explanation of a Bible passage) on Moses' being veiled when he came *from* the presence of God, whereas he was unveiled when he entered the tent of the Presence. Believers are those who now turn to the Lord, who is here equated with the Spirit of the Lord, the key to God's presence in the present age. As with Moses, but now by the Spirit, we are unveiled as we enter the sanctuary to behold the glory of the Lord.

It is the play on veil and Spirit that makes the argument so telling; the Spirit of the Presence has now removed the veil—most likely also alluding to the veil keeping people away from God's presence within the temple. The result is that by the Spirit's coming, the veil is removed, both from our faces and from the Presence, so that we can behold the glory of the Lord himself in the face of God's Son, our Lord Jesus Christ.

Here Paul enters the holy place. By the Spirit's presence one is now behind the veil in the very presence of God, not only beholding God's glory in Christ but also being transformed into God's likeness from one degree of glory to another. Here the *Abba*-cry evolves into praise and adoration. Here too God's children are transformed from the likeness of their former "father," the god of this world who still blinds the hearts of those who do not believe (4:4), into the likeness of God himself (3:18). We now bear his image in our present "already but not yet" existence.[14] This is not the only thing Paul believes the Spirit to be doing in our present world, but it is very significant, and we miss Paul by a wide margin if we do not pay close attention to it.

In sum: For Paul, the Spirit is not merely an impersonal force or influence or power. The Spirit is none other than the fulfillment of the promise that God himself would once again be present with his people. The implications of this are considerable, not only in terms of Paul's understanding of God and the Spirit (the concern of the next two chapters), but in terms of what it means for us individually and corporately to be the people of God (the concern of chs. 6-14). The Spirit is God's own personal presence in our lives and in our midst; he leads us into paths of righteousness for his name's sake, he "is working all things in all people," he is grieved when his people do not reflect his character and thus reveal his glory, and he is present in our worship, as we sing "praise and honor and glory and power" to God and the Lamb.

It is for God's people of a later time like ours once more to grasp these realities *by experiencing them,* if we are truly to capture Paul's understanding. Perhaps a beginning point for us would be to downplay the impersonal images (wind, fire, etc.), as rich as they are in terms of aspects of the Spirit's ministry, and to retool our thinking in Paul's own terms, where we understand and experience the Spirit as the personal presence of the eternal God. That is where the next two chapters fit in.

NOTES

1. As prophesied by Joel (Joel 2:28-30). Paul viewed this as the primary way the Spirit is present in the gathered community; see 1 Thess 5:19-22; 1 Cor 11:4-5; 12:1-14:40; Rom 12:6; 1 Tim 4:14. See also the discussion in ch. 14 below.

2. On this matter see especially the discussion of 2 Cor 3:4–6 and Rom 2:29 in *GEP*; see also the discussion in ch. 9 below (pp. 100–104).

3. On the theme of the divine presence as the key to biblical theology, see Samuel Terrien, *The Elusive Presence: Toward a New Biblical Theology* (San Francisco: Harper & Row, 1978).

4. On the significance of this motif for Paul, see the discussion on pp. 59–61 below.

5. For example, see the apocalyptic writer of *1 Enoch* ("After this, the Righteous and Elect One will reveal the house of his congregation," 53:6; "I went on seeing until the Lord of the sheep brought about a new house, greater and loftier than the first one," 90:29).

6. This is my own translation, although I have deliberately followed the language of the NIV or NRSV as much as possible. For v. 9 in particular, also following the NRSV, see *GEP*, 713–14.

7. It should be noted that in the Gospels of Matthew and John, Christ plays this role. In Matthew 1, for example, Zechariah is told that Jesus' name will be "Immanuel," that is, "God with us"; in ch. 12 Jesus, referring to himself, says that "something greater than the temple is here"; and the Gospel concludes with the Risen Lord telling the disciples, "I am with you always, even to the end of the age." In John 1:14 the "Word" is said to "have tabernacled among us," so that "we beheld his glory, the glory of the one and only Son of the Father," who himself was full of the Father's attributes of "grace and truth [faithfulness]." The trinitarian implications of both Christ and the Spirit as fulfilling the renewed presence motif will be spelled out in ch. 4 below.

8. See the exegesis of these various passages in *GEP*.

9. See the discussion of this passage in *GEP*, 50–53, where the unusual Greek expression, translated "who gives his Spirit *into* you," is best understood as coming from the Septuagint reading of Ezek 36:27 and 37:14.

10. For the exegesis supporting the conclusions expressed here, see *GEP*, 112–18.

11. Paul has just made the point that the Spirit whom they have received is also the one who reveals to us the wisdom in "God's folly," the cross (2:10; cf. 1:18–25); in 12:13 he will state that the Spirit makes the many of them, in all their diversity, one body in 12:13.

12. On the further theological implications of this passage, see pp. 58–59 below.

13. For the full exegesis of the Spirit passages in this larger section, see *GEP*, 296–321.

14. For this language, see ch. 5 below.

THE HOLY WHO?
THE SPIRIT AS PERSON

*As fulfillment of the renewed presence of God
with his people, the Spirit was understood
by Paul in personal terms.*

A student once told a colleague of mine: "God the Father makes perfectly good sense to me; and God the Son I can quite understand; but the Holy Spirit is a gray, oblong blur." How many of God's people can empathize! Most Christians have little trouble relating to the Father and the Son because of the personal images involved and the reality of the incarnation—even though they know that God is Spirit (John 4:24). But it is otherwise with the Spirit, where Christian understanding falls considerably short of personhood.

This point was illustrated vividly for me during the children's time on Pentecost Sunday a few years ago. A good friend was trying to portray the reality of "Spirit" by blowing on a piece of paper and letting it "fly" away. The Spirit is like that, she was saying to the children; it is like the "wind,"[1] very real in its visible effects, even though the wind itself is invisible. At which point a six-year-old boy blurted out, "But I want the wind to be un-invisible!"

"Exactly!" I whispered to my wife, Maudine. "What a profound moment!" How often we all feel this way about God as Spirit, as Holy Spirit. "I want the Holy Spirit to be un-invisible!" And because he is not, because we see the effects but have no personal images, we tend to think of the Spirit in nonpersonal terms and refer to him as "it." Listen to our images: dove, wind, fire, water, oil. No wonder many regard the Spirit as a gray, oblong blur and find him so difficult to understand and to relate to. To paraphrase the creed, "We believe in God the Father, Almighty, Maker of heaven and earth; and we believe in Jesus Christ his Son; but we are not so sure about the Holy Spirit."

Listen to our images:

dove, wind, fire,

water, oil. No wonder

many regard the Spirit

as a gray, oblong blur

and find him so

difficult to understand

and to relate to.

Our understanding of God is forever marked by the fact that in Christ he has been "fleshed out" at one point in our human history. Even if God seems distant, transcendent, "from eternity to eternity," we are not in the dark about God and his character. As Paul put it, the glory of God has been imaged for us in the one true human who bears the divine image, Christ himself; and by beholding his "face" we see the glory of the eternal God (2 Cor 3:18; 4:4, 6).

The concern of this chapter is that we must recognize the same to be true about the Spirit, not simply theoretically but really and experientially. The Spirit is not lightly called the Spirit of Jesus Christ. Christ has put a human face on the Spirit as well. Not only has the coming of Christ changed everything for Paul, so too has the coming of the Spirit. In dealing with the Spirit, we are dealing with none other than the *personal* presence of God.

THE HOLY SPIRIT AS PERSON

Even though Paul does not speak directly to the question of the Spirit's person, several converging pieces of evidence assure us that he understood the Spirit in personal terms, intimately associated with both the Father and the Son, yet distinct from them.

First, we must acknowledge that the Spirit is most frequently spoken of in terms of *agency*—that is, the Spirit is the *agent* of God's activity. It is also true that such language does not necessarily presume personhood. Nonetheless, even a casual glance at the passages where Paul refers to the Spirit (or Holy Spirit) shows how often agency finds personal expression.[2] For instance, the Thessalonians' conversion is by the sanctifying work of the Spirit (2 Thess 2:13; cf. 1 Cor 6:11; Rom 15:16), as is their accompanying joy (1 Thess 1:6; cf. Rom 15:13). Revelation comes through the Spirit (1 Cor 2:10; Eph 3:5); and Paul's preaching is accompanied by the power of the Spirit (1 Thess 1:5). Prophetic speech and speaking in tongues result directly from speaking by the Spirit (1 Cor 12:3; 14:2, 16). By the Spirit the Romans are to put to death any sinful practices (Rom 8:13). Paul desires the Ephesians to be strengthened by means of God's Spirit (Eph 3:16). Believers serve by the Spirit (Phil 3:3), love by the Spirit (Col 1:8), are sealed by the Spirit (Eph 1:13), and walk and live by the Spirit (Gal 5:16, 25). Finally, believers are "saved through washing by the Spirit, whom God poured out upon them" (Titus 3:5).

On the one hand, a passage like the last one might suggest agency in quite impersonal terms. The concept of "pouring out" does not bring to mind the idea of personhood; neither does the imagery of "washing" by the Spirit. On the other hand, a careful look at most of these passages and others indicates that personhood is either implied or presupposed, and that the language of "pouring out" is imagery, pure and simple. This is especially evident in a passage like 1 Corinthians 6:11, where God "washes, justifies, and sanctifies" by the double agency of "the name [authority] of the Lord Jesus Christ" and "by the Spirit of our God."

The point to make is that what Paul says of the Spirit in terms of agency parallels what he says in scores of places about Christ, whose agency can only be personal. By implication, the Spirit's agency can hardly be less personal than that of Christ. Moreover, one is struck by the scarcity of impersonal images in Paul's letters. In contrast to Luke, he seldom speaks of being filled with the Spirit; his primary language has to do with God's "giving his Spirit into you,"[3] or of our "receiving" or "having" the Spirit.[4] None of these images implies personhood, but neither do they imply what is impersonal, as so many other Spirit images do (wind, fire, etc.). That Paul understands the Spirit as *person* is confirmed, secondly, by the fact that the Spirit is the subject of a large number of verbs that demand a personal agent: The Spirit *searches* all things (1 Cor 2:10), *knows* the mind of God (1 Cor 2:11), *teaches* the content of the gospel to believers (1 Cor 2:13), *dwells* among or within believers (1 Cor 3:16; Rom 8:11; 2 Tim 1:14), *accomplishes* all things (1 Cor 12:11), *gives life* to those who believe (2 Cor 3:6), *cries out* from within our hearts (Gal 4:6), *leads* us in the ways of God (Gal 5:18; Rom 8:14), *bears witness* with our own spirits (Rom 8:16), *has desires* that are in opposition to the flesh (Gal 5:17), *helps* us in our weakness (Rom 8:26), *intercedes* in our behalf (Rom 8:26–27), *works* all things *together* for our ultimate good (Rom 8:28),[5] *strengthens* believers (Eph 3:16), and is *grieved* by our sinfulness (Eph 4:30). Furthermore, the fruit of the Spirit's indwelling are the personal attributes of God (Gal 5:22–23).

Some of these texts seem to clinch the question of Spirit as person, as for example Romans 8:16. The Spirit who gives us "adoption as sons," attested by his prompting within us the "*Abba*-cry," in turn, and for this reason, becomes the second (necessary) witness[6] along with our own spirits to the reality of our being God's children. Likewise in Romans 8:26–27, not only does the Spirit intercede in our behalf, thus "knowing us" being implied, but we can be assured of the effectiveness of his intercession because "God knows *the mind* of the Spirit," who in turn thus prays "according to God['s will]." Whatever else, this is the language of personhood, not that of an impersonal influence or power. The term *pneuma* may have the imagery of "wind" inherent in it, but Paul never uses it in this manner.

Finally, the Spirit is sometimes the subject of a verb or implied activity that elsewhere is attributed either to the Father or to the Son. For example, in successive passages in 1 Corinthians 12 Paul says of God (the Father is implied) that he "produces" all these activities in all people (*panta en pasin*, v. 6), while in a similar sentence in v. 11 the Spirit is the subject of the identical verb with a similar object (*panta tauta*, "all these things," now referring to the

many Spirit manifestations enumerated in vv. 8–10). Likewise, in
Romans 8:11 the Father "gives life," while in 2 Corinthians 3:6 it is
the Spirit; and in Romans 8:34 Christ "intercedes" for us, while a few
verses earlier (8:26) this was said of the Spirit. Similarly, but now
with the Spirit as the object of the verb, in consecutive sentences in
Galatians 4:5–6 Paul asserts that "God sent forth his Son" and that
"God sent forth the Spirit of his Son" (cf. 1 Cor 6:11). Both the
parallel and the fact that the activities of the Son and of the Spirit
(redemption and crying out from within the heart of the believer)
are personal activities presuppose the Spirit as person.

This evidence indicates clearly that for Paul the Spirit is not
thought of as "it," but as "person." But what does this mean in
terms of the nature of God? What is the relationship between the
Spirit and God and Christ? Is the language of the later church,
"one with, but distinct from" the other two persons of the Trinity,
a proper way of expressing Paul's understanding? This last issue,
and its implications for the contemporary church, will be taken up
in the next chapter. We conclude this chapter by noting the relationship between the Spirit and God and Christ, which not only
further indicates that the Spirit is personal, but also leads us into
the next chapter by pointing us in the direction of historical
orthodoxy (that is, unity of substance along with distinction of
persons in the Trinity).

THE SPIRIT AND THE GODHEAD

Of over 140 occurrences of *pneuma* ("S/spirit") in his letters, Paul
uses the full name, Holy Spirit, in seventeen instances. He designates the Spirit as "the Spirit of God"/"his Spirit" sixteen times,
and as "the Spirit of Christ," or its equivalent, three times. Some
observations about this usage are in order.

The Holy Spirit

This full designation occurs only twice in the Old Testament (Ps
51:11; Isa 63:10); nonetheless, it was picked up by Christians as

the full proper name for the Spirit of God. For all practical purposes, it came to be understood as the Spirit's "Christian" name. Paul uses the full name at about the same ratio as he uses of his full name for Christ, "the Lord Jesus Christ," where name and title also blend as one reality. This usage in itself, and especially in a passage like 2 Corinthians 13:14 (see ch. 4 below), further indicates that "distinct from" and "one with" is the Pauline presupposition about the Spirit.

The Spirit as the Spirit of God

Despite the fact that his understanding of the Spirit has been forever stamped by the coming of Christ, Paul nonetheless thinks of the Spirit primarily in terms of the Spirit's relationship to God (the Father).[7] Not only does he speak more often of the "Spirit of God" than of the "Spirit of Christ," but God is invariably the subject of the verb when Paul speaks of a person's receiving the Spirit. For example, God "sent forth the Spirit of his Son into our hearts" (Gal 4:6), and God "gives" us his Spirit (1 Thess 4:8; 2 Cor 1:22; 5:5; Gal 3:5; Rom 5:5; Eph 1:17). This understanding is surely determined by Paul's Old Testament roots, where God "fills with" (Exod 31:3) or "pours out" his Spirit (Joel 2:28), and the Spirit of God comes on people for all sorts of extraordinary (charismatic) activities (e.g., Num 24:2; Judg 3:10).

Two passages in particular give insight into Paul's understanding of this primary, foundational relationship between God (the Father) and the Spirit. In 1 Corinthians 2:10–12 he uses the analogy of human interior consciousness (only one's "spirit" knows one's mind) to insist that the Spirit alone knows the mind of God. Paul's concern in this analogy is with the Spirit whom the Corinthians have received as the source of our Christian understanding of the cross as God's wisdom; nonetheless, the analogy itself draws the closest kind of relationship between God and the Spirit. The Spirit alone "searches all things," even "the depths of God"; and because of this unique relationship with God, the Spirit alone knows and reveals God's otherwise hidden wisdom (1 Cor 2:7).

In Romans 8:26–27 this same idea is expressed in reverse: God knows the mind of the Spirit. Among other matters, Paul is here concerned to show how the Spirit, in the presence of our weaknesses and inability to speak for ourselves, is able to intercede adequately on our behalf. The effectiveness of the Spirit's intercession lies precisely in the fact that God, who searches our hearts, likewise "knows the mind of the Spirit," who is interceding for us.

The Spirit is both the interior expression of the unseen God's personality and the visible manifestation of God's activity in the world.

Some mystery is involved here, because finally we are dealing with divine mysteries. There can be little question that Paul sees the Spirit as distinct from God; yet at the same time the Spirit is both the interior expression of the unseen God's personality and the visible manifestation of God's activity in the world. The Spirit is truly God in action; yet he is neither simply an outworking of God's personality nor all there is to say about God.

The Spirit "of God/of Christ"

Given the preceding texts, the cause for wonder is that Paul should *also* refer to the Spirit as "the Spirit of Christ." That he does so at all says something far more significant about his view of Christ than about his view of the Spirit—although the latter is significant as well. Here is evidence for Paul's high Christology (his understanding of Christ as fully God): that Paul, steeped in the Old Testament understanding of the Spirit of God, should so easily, on the basis of his Christian experience, speak of him as the Spirit of Christ as well.

A careful analysis of all the texts in which Paul identifies the Spirit either as "the Spirit of God" or as "the Spirit of Christ" suggests that he customarily chose to use the qualifier "of God/Christ" when he wanted to emphasize the activity of either God or Christ that is being conveyed to the believer by the Spirit. Thus the church is God's temple because the Spirit "of God" dwells in its midst (1 Cor 3:16); or God gives his Holy Spirit to those he calls to be holy (1 Thess 4:8).

So also in the three texts in which the Spirit is called the Spirit of Christ, the emphasis lies on the work of Christ. In Galatians 4:6 the emphasis is on the believers' "sonship," evidenced by their having received "the Spirit of God's Son," through whom they use the Son's language to address God. In Romans 8:9 Paul seems to be deliberately tying together the work of Christ in chapter 6 with that of the Spirit in chapter 8, hence the evidence that they are truly God's people is that they are indwelt by the Spirit of Christ. And in Philippians 1:19 Paul desires a fresh supply of the Spirit of Christ Jesus so that when he is on trial, Christ will be magnified, whether by life or by death.

All this suggests that Paul uses these "of God/Christ" qualifiers to indicate relationship or identification. That is, the Spirit to whom Paul is referring is the Spirit who is to be understood in terms of his relationship either with God or with Christ. "God" and "Christ" in each case give identity to the Spirit, in terms of what relationship Paul is referring to.

Finally, in Romans 8:9-11 Paul distinctly and absolutely identifies "the Spirit of God" with "the Spirit of Christ." He is referring to the one Holy Spirit, who elsewhere is the Spirit of God. In this text especially the unity of Father, Son, and Spirit is made certain. It remains only to explore briefly the relationship between Christ and the Spirit.

The Spirit as the Spirit of Christ

As noted earlier, in Christian theology in general and Paul's theology in particular, the coming of Christ has forever marked our understanding of God. The transcendent God of the universe is henceforth known as "the father of our Lord Jesus Christ" (2 Cor 1:3; Eph 1:3; 1 Pet 1:3), who "sent his Son" into the world to redeem us (Gal 4:4-5). Likewise the coming of Christ has forever marked our understanding of the Spirit. The Spirit of God is also the Spirit of Christ (Gal 4:6; Rom 8:9; Phil 1:19), who carries on the work of Christ following his resurrection and subsequent assumption of the place of authority at God's right hand. To have received the Spirit of God (1 Cor 2:12) is to have the mind of Christ (v. 16).

For Paul, therefore, Christ gives a fuller definition to the Spirit: Spirit people are God's children, fellow heirs with God's Son (Rom 8:14–17); they simultaneously know the power of Christ's resurrection and the fellowship of his sufferings (Phil 3:10); at the same time Christ is the absolute criterion for what is truly Spirit activity (e.g., 1 Cor 12:3). Thus it is fair to say with some that Paul's doctrine of the Spirit is Christ-centered, in the sense that Christ and his work help define the Spirit and his work in the Christian life.

But some have pressed this relationship further, and in so doing have seemed to miss Paul's own perspective. Based chiefly on three texts (1 Cor 6:17; 15:45; 2 Cor 3:17–18),[8] Paul is understood to speak of the risen Lord in such a way as to identify him with the Spirit. The main text is 2 Corinthians 3:17–18, where Paul's language, "the Lord is the Spirit," seems to imply some sort of identification. In context, however, Paul is using a well-known form of Jewish interpretation, in which the interpreter picks out one word from a biblical citation and gives its "true meaning" for a new context. Thus "the Lord is the Spirit" interprets "the Lord" just mentioned in v. 16, which is an allusion to Exodus 34:34. The "Lord" to whom we turn, Paul says, has to do with the Spirit. That is, "the Lord" is now to be understood in terms of the Spirit's activity among us—the Spirit of the new covenant, who brings freedom and transforms God's people into "the glory of the Lord." Similarly, in the case of both 1 Corinthians 6:17 and 15:45 the language has been dictated by their contexts, where contrasts set up by the argument call forth the usage. Neither of these passages identifies the Spirit with the risen Lord.

That the risen Christ and the Spirit are clearly distinct from one another in Paul's thinking is demonstrated from all kinds of evidence. Besides the passages discussed in the next chapter that imply the Trinity, other texts indicate that the activities of the risen Christ and the Spirit are kept separate in his understanding. This is true of passages as diverse as Romans 9:1, where the formula "in Christ" and "by the Spirit" function quite differently—but characteristically—in one sentence,[9] and Romans

15:30 ("through our Lord Jesus Christ and through the love of the Spirit"), where the repeated Greek preposition *dia* ("through") indicates the twofold basis of Paul's appeal. First, it is "through our Lord Jesus Christ," meaning "on the basis of what Christ has done for us all as outlined in the argument of this letter"; second, it is "through the love of the Spirit," meaning "on the basis of the love for all the saints, including myself, that the Spirit engenders."

Perhaps the most significant text in this regard, thinking only of passages where Christ and the Spirit appear in close proximity, is the combination of Romans 8:26–27 (the Spirit intercedes for us) and 8:34 (Christ intercedes for us). On the surface one could argue for identification in function; but what we really get is the clearest expression of distinction. The role of the Spirit is on earth, indwelling believers in order to help them in the weakness of their present "already/not yet" existence and thereby to intercede in their behalf. The risen Christ is "located" in heaven, "at the right hand of God, making intercession for us."[10] This text in particular, where Paul is not arguing for something but asserting it on the basis of a presupposed reality, negates altogether the idea that the Spirit in Paul's mind is to be identified with the risen Christ, either in essence or in function.

Nonetheless, although Paul does not identify the Spirit and Christ, he does assume the same kind of close relationship between the two as exists between the Spirit and God. Thus at times he moves easily from the mention of the one to the other, especially when using the language of indwelling (e.g., Rom 8:9–10, from "have the Spirit of Christ" to "Christ is in you"; cf. Eph 3:16–17). Accordingly, when Paul in Galatians 2:20 speaks of Christ as living in him, he almost certainly means "Christ lives in me by his Spirit," referring to the ongoing work of Christ in his life that is being carried out by the indwelling Spirit.

This fluid use of language most likely results from the fact that Paul's concern with both Christ and the Spirit is not with the nature of their being God, but with their role in salvation and Christian experience. It is in examining this concern of Paul's that we meet the Trinity in his writings; and to this matter we turn in chapter 4.

In sum: Whatever else, in Paul's thinking and experience, the Holy Spirit is not some kind of "it," an impersonal force that comes from God. The Spirit is fully personal, indeed, in the language of a later time, "God very God."

The implications of this for the contemporary church are enormous. Whereas we pay lip service to this reality in our trinitarian confessions, in practice the majority of Christians tend toward believing in the "oblong blur" of my young student friend of many years ago. The result is that the implications of the renewed presence of God by his Spirit, noted in the preceding chapter, scarcely inspire believers in one direction or the other. Surely the reality that God is personally present in and among us should encourage us through the exigencies and weaknesses of our present life, not to mention revitalize us when our shoulders droop and our hands grow weary.

> We must not merely cite the creed, but believe and experience the presence of God in the person of the Spirit.

The coming of the Holy Spirit in and among us means that the living God, in the person of the Spirit, is indeed with us. And he is present, as we will point out in later chapters, as an *empowering* presence. Here, then, is one of the shifts that must take place in our thinking and experience if we are to be biblical, and thus more effective, in our postmodern world. We must not merely cite the creed, but believe and experience the presence of God in the person of the Spirit.

NOTES

1. Both Greek *pneuma* and Hebrew *rûaḥ* can mean either "spirit" or "wind," depending on context (cf. the play on this usage in John 3:5).

2. For a list of these passages in their various formulations, see ch. 2 in *GEP*.

3. See *GEP* on 1 Thess 4:8; cf. 2 Cor 1:22; 5:5; Rom 5:5; Eph 1:17; 2 Tim 1:7; cf. "the supply of the Spirit" in Gal 3:5 and Phil 1:19.

4. For "receive" see *GEP* on 1 Cor 2:12; 2 Cor 11:4; Gal 3:2, 14; Rom 8:15; for "have" see 1 Cor 2:16; 7:40; Rom 8:9.

5. For this understanding of Rom 8:28, see *GEP*, 587-90.

6. That is, Paul is reflecting his biblical heritage that everything shall be established by two or three witnesses (Deut 19:15); cf. 2 Cor 13:1.

7. It should be noted that, unless otherwise specified, the word "God" in Paul always refers to God the Father.

8. For a full exegesis of these three texts, see the appropriate places in *GEP*. Some also appeal to Rom 1:3-4 and 8:9-10 (see, e.g., N. Q. Hamilton, *The Holy Spirit and Eschatology in Paul* [SJTOP 6; Edinburgh: Oliver & Boyd, 1957] 10-15); however, these texts do not suggest any identification; indeed, they demonstrate the opposite. See the discussions in *GEP*, ch. 7.

9. See *GEP*, 833 n. 19.

10. Cf. Arthur W. Wainwright, *The Trinity in the New Testament* (London: SPCK, 1962) 260.

GOD IN THREE PERSONS—THE SPIRIT AND THE TRINITY

*Along with their experience of Christ, the experience
of the Spirit as the renewed presence of God
expanded the earliest Christians' and Paul's
understanding of the one God as triune.*

Rose was a nominal Christian, who in her adult years had basically abandoned any relationship to the Christian faith. One day two people came to her door with a new brand of "Christianity," which in truth was nothing new at all. The Jehovah's Witnesses who visited her were self-aware Arians,[1] who not only deny the deity of Christ but have no knowledge or experience of the Spirit as the personal presence of God. They offered Rose a simplistic faith, one in which the mystery of the Trinity was removed; and in her own spiritual emptiness she bought it—hook, line, and sinker.

In a long afternoon of conversation with Rose and two of the leaders from her Kingdom Hall, my son Mark and I carefully went through all the christological texts with them—texts with which they were familiar, albeit in a superficial and rote way—but continually reached dead ends. Toward the end of the afternoon, however, Mark asked them about their experience of the Holy Spirit. They drew a total blank. The "holy spirit" was for them no person at all, but only an "influence" from God in our behalf. When we began to describe our life in the Spirit, they became noticeably ill at ease, and the conversation came to a speedy end. Not only had we begun to enter an area where they had no trained response; but also the one essential ingredient to their becoming believers in Christ was clearly missing—the pouring out of the Spirit into their lives so as to cry "*Abba,* Father" to Jehovah.

Through that experience I became convinced that the reason Rose, and so many others like her, get trapped by this present-day Arianism is only in part because the Trinity is a mystery (most people, after all, prefer to reduce God to a size that their own minds can grasp, and thus control); it is also because they have been let down by the church, which continually treats the Spirit as a matter of creed and doctrine, but not as a vital experienced reality in believers' lives.

Indeed, on this matter, the Jehovah's Witnesses are abetted by a large number of New Testament scholars. Some deny that Paul was a trinitarian at all; others, even among those who are very orthodox, are skittish of using the language of "Trinity" to describe the New Testament witness. Part of the problem here is one of definitions. "Trinity" is the language of later thinkers, who landed on this word to express the church's faith in the one God, whom they knew to be a unity of three divine Persons.[2] Thus it is common to assert that if the New Testament reflects "trinitarianism," it does so in an embryonic way, so that, whatever else, it was not the trinitarianism of a later day such as Chalcedon.[3] But that seems so self-evident that one wonders why it needs to have been repeated so often. The problem with such wariness is that its frequent repetition finally comes home to roost—such protests too often lead to practical denial.

We are led to wonder, then, whether our difficulties with the Trinity do not stem in part from our own experience of the church and the Spirit, where the Spirit is understood not as person but as divine influence or power. After all, it is a short step from our experience of the Spirit as a "gray, oblong blur" to our becoming practical binitarians.[4] As noted earlier, the practicing creed for many Christians goes something like, "I believe in God the Father; I believe in Jesus Christ, God's Son; but I wonder about the Holy Ghost." The Spirit has become God's specter, if you will, an unseen, less than vibrant influence, hardly "God very God."

The concern of this chapter is that Paul was trinitarian at the core of his experience and theology, and that such a trinitarian understanding makes a difference in our own relationship to God.

PAUL AND THE TRINITY

To be sure, Paul's experience and understanding of the Spirit as God's personal presence inevitably leads us into some deep theological waters. At issue for us is *how* God exists in his essential being as triune. How can God be known as Father, Son, and Spirit, one being, yet each "person" distinct from the other? We tend to think that a person is not a true trinitarian unless that person has a working formulation in response to this question.

Paul was trinitarian at the core of his experience and theology.

To put the question this way, however, is to get ahead of Paul, not to mention to define trinitarianism by later standards. What makes this an issue for us at all is that Paul, the strictest of monotheists, who never doubted that "the Lord thy God is one," wrote letters to his churches that are full of presuppositions and assertions which reveal that he *experienced* God, and then expressed that experience, in a fundamentally trinitarian way.

That he does not deal with the theological issues this trinitarianism would pose for a monotheistic Jew only points again to Paul's letters as practical rather than theological documents. Paul was writing not to present a study of God, but to build up churches and address gut issues about their being God's people in a totally pagan environment. He was too busy being a missionary pastor to have the luxury of purely reflective theology. Thus Paul affirms, asserts, and presupposes the Trinity in every way; and those affirmations—that the one God known and experienced as Father, Son, and Holy Spirit, each distinct from the other, is yet only one God—are precisely the reason the later church took up the question of how.

The affirmations stem first from his experience of the risen Christ as "Lord," the Old Testament language for God, about whom he spoke as the preexistent Son of God (e.g., 2 Cor 8:9; Gal 4:6–7) and to whom he attributed every imaginable activity that Paul's Judaism reserved for God alone. In contrast to pagan polytheism, Paul asserts, "for us there is only one God, the Father, and only one Lord, Jesus Christ" (1 Cor 8:6); yet at the end of the ages, when the final victory of death is won through our resurrection, the Son turns it all over to the Father so that the one God "may be all in all" (1 Cor 15:28).

Given such affirmations and assertions, there can be little question that the early church would have finally expressed itself in a *bi*nitarian way had it never done so in a *tri*nitarian way. That the issue is Trinity, not binity, comes directly out of the church's personal encounter with God through the Spirit as put forth in the preceding two chapters.

At issue, therefore, and our present concern, is what Paul believed about the Spirit, since the Trinity expresses the Christian conviction about God not only as one being in three *persons,* but as one God in *three* persons, including God the Holy Spirit. The question is, Did Paul in fact have a trinitarian faith, even if he did not use the language of a later time to describe God? Analysis of the Pauline data suggests that he did.[5]

THE SPIRIT AND THE TRINITY

At the heart of Paul's theology is his gospel, and his gospel is essentially about *salvation*—God's saving a people for his name through the redeeming work of Christ and the applying work of the Spirit. Paul's encounter with God in salvation, as Father, Son, and Holy Spirit, alone accounts for the transformation of his theological language and of his understanding of God.[6] In light of this reality and the great number of texts that support it—with trinitarian language—these passages rightly serve as the starting point for any study of the Trinity in Paul.

The evidence here is found in two sets of texts: several explicitly trinitarian texts (2 Cor 13:14; 1 Cor 12:4–6; Eph 4:4–6) and the many passages where Paul encapsulates "salvation in Christ" in trinitarian terms, sometimes in semicreedal fashion, but always in nonreflective, presuppositional ways.

The Trinitarian Texts

The remarkable grace-benediction of 2 Corinthians 13:14 offers us all kinds of theological keys to Paul's understanding of salvation and of God himself.[7] That the benediction is composed and intended for the occasion rather than as a broadly applicable formula only increases its importance in hearing Paul. Thus what he says here in prayer appears in a thoroughly presuppositional way—not as something he argues for, but as the assumed, experienced reality of Christian life.

First, it summarizes the core elements of Paul's unique passion: the gospel, with its focus on salvation in Christ, equally available by faith to Gentile and Jew alike. That the *love of God* is the foundation of Paul's view of salvation is stated with passion and clarity in passages such as Romans 5:1–11, 8:31–39, and Ephesians 1:3–14. The *grace of our Lord Jesus Christ* is what gave concrete expression to that love; through Christ's suffering and death on behalf of his loved ones, God accomplished salvation for them at one moment in human history.

The *participation in the Holy Spirit* continually makes that love and grace real in the life of the believer and the believing community. The *koinōnia* ("fellowship/participation") *of the Holy Spirit* (note the full name!) is how the living God not only brings people into an intimate and abiding relationship with himself, as the God of all grace, but also causes them to participate in all the benefits of that grace and salvation—that is, by indwelling them in the present with his own presence and guaranteeing their final eschatological glory.

Second, this text also serves as our entrée into Paul's understanding of God, which had been so radically affected for him by the twin realities of the death and resurrection of Christ and the gift of the Spirit. Granted, Paul does not here assert the deity of Christ and the Spirit. What he does is to equate the activity of the three divine Persons (to use the language of a later time) in concert and in one prayer, with the clause about God the Father standing in second place. This suggests that Paul was truly trinitarian in any meaningful sense of that term—that the one God is Father, Son, and Spirit, and that when dealing with Christ and the Spirit one is dealing with God every bit as much as when one is dealing with the Father. Thus this benediction, while making a fundamental distinction among God, Christ, and Spirit, also expresses in short-hand form what is found throughout his letters, namely, that "salvation in Christ" is the cooperative work of God, Christ, and the Spirit.[8]

The same fully trinitarian implications appear in 1 Corinthians 12:4-6 and Ephesians 4:4-6. In the former passage Paul urges the Corinthians to broaden their perspective and to recognize the rich diversity of the Spirit's manifestations in their midst (over against their apparently singular interest in speaking in tongues). He begins in vv. 4-6 by noting that diversity reflects the nature of God and is therefore the true evidence of the work of the one God in their midst. Thus the Trinity is presuppositional to the entire argument, and it is the more telling precisely because it is so unstudied, so freely and unconsciously expressed.

In Ephesians 4:4-6 one finds the same combination as in 2 Corinthians 13:14—a creedal formulation expressed in terms of the distinguishable activities of the triune God. The basis for Christian unity is the one God. The one body is the work of the one Spirit (cf. 1 Cor 12:13), by whom also we live our present eschatological existence in one hope, since the Spirit is the "down payment on our inheritance" (Eph 1:13-14). All of this has been made possible for us by our one Lord, in whom all have one faith and to which faith all have given witness through one baptism. The source of all these realities is the one God himself, "who is over all and through all and in all."

If the last phrase in this passage reemphasizes the unity of the one God, who is ultimately responsible for all things—past, present, and future—and subsumes the work of the Spirit and the Son under that of God, the entire passage at the same time puts into creedal form the affirmation that God is *experienced* as a triune reality. Precisely on the basis of such experience and language the later church maintained its biblical integrity by expressing all of this in explicitly trinitarian language. Paul's formulations, which include the work of the Spirit, form part of that basis.

Salvation in Christ as the Work of the Trinity

That the work of the Trinity in salvation is foundational to Paul's understanding of the gospel is further evidenced by the many texts that formulate salvation in less explicit, but fully presuppositionally trinitarian terms. This is especially true of passages such as Romans 5:1–8; 2 Corinthians 3:1–4:6; Galatians 4:4–6; or Ephesians 1:3–14 (cf. Titus 3:4–7).

As an example, we may take Romans 5:1–8. As everywhere, the Spirit plays a vital role in Paul's and his churches' experience of God's saving grace. For Paul the "love of God" was no mere abstraction. God's love, the most essential reality about his character and the absolute predicate of our existence, has been demonstrated historically in its most lavish and expansive expression through Christ's death for his enemies (vv. 6–8, thus the basis for "peace with God" and "access" to his gracious presence). But such love is not merely an objective historical event. By the presence of the Spirit, God's love, played out to the full in Christ, is an experienced reality in the heart of the believer. *This* is what the Spirit has so richly "shed abroad in our hearts."

For Paul the "love of God" was no mere abstraction.

If we are not thus overtaken by God himself at this crucial point, then all else is lost, and we are without peace, groveling before God, living with little real hope, and experiencing present sufferings as a cause for complaint and despair rather than for "boasting." What rectifies all of this for us is not simply the fact of God's love—although in some ways that would surely be enough—but that God's love has been effectively realized in the experience of the believer. God's love for us has been "poured out" as a prodigal, experienced reality by the presence of the Holy Spirit, whom God has also lavishly poured out into our hearts.[9]

But besides these grand, well-known moments in Paul, this trinitarian understanding of salvation is also evident in many other texts that portray salvation as the threefold work of the triune God, as encapsulated in 2 Corinthians 13:14:[10]

— First Thessalonians 1:4–5, where the love of God has made election effective through the gospel (the message about Christ) empowered by the Holy Spirit.

— Second Thessalonians 2:13, where God's people are "beloved by the Lord (through his death)," because God elected them for salvation through the sanctifying work of the Spirit.

— First Corinthians 1:4–7, where God's grace has been given in Christ Jesus, who in turn has enriched the church with every kind of Spirit gifting.

— First Corinthians 2:4–5, where Paul's preaching of Christ crucified (v. 2) is accompanied by the Spirit's power so that the Corinthians' faith might rest in God.

— First Corinthians 2:12, where "we have received the Spirit that comes from God," so that we might know the things given to us ("in the cross" is implied in context) by God.

— First Corinthians 6:11, where God is the implied subject of the "divine passives" (you were washed, justified, sanctified), accomplished in the name of Christ and by the Spirit.

— First Corinthians 6:19–20, where the believer has been purchased (by Christ; cf. 7:22–23) so as to become a temple for God's presence by the Spirit.

— Second Corinthians 1:21–22, where God is the one who has "confirmed" believers in a salvation accomplished by Christ, God's "Yes" (vv. 19–20), proved by his giving the Spirit as "down payment."

— Galatians 3:1–5, where Christ crucified (v. 1, picking up on 2:16–21) is conveyed to believers by the Spirit, whom God yet "supplies" among them (v. 5).

— Romans 8:3–4, where God sent his Son to do what the law could not do in terms of securing salvation, and the Spirit does what the law could not do in terms of accomplishing righteous behavior in the believer's life ("walking" = living in the ways of God).

— Romans 8:15–17, where the God-given Spirit serves as evidence of "adoption" as children, and thus "joint heirs" with Christ, who made it all possible.

— Colossians 3:16, where in worship it is all played in reverse: as the message of Christ "dwells richly among them," they worship the God from whom salvation has come, by means of Spirit-inspired songs.

— Ephesians 1:17, where the God of our Lord Jesus Christ gives the Spirit of wisdom and revelation so that they may understand the full measure of the work of Christ in their behalf.

— Ephesians 2:18, where "through [the death of] Christ" (vv. 14–16) Jew and Gentile together have access to God by the one Spirit, whom both alike have received.

— Ephesians 2:20–22, where Christ is the "cornerstone" for the new temple, the place of God's dwelling by his Spirit.

— Philippians 3:3, where believers serve ("God" is implied) by the Spirit of God and thus boast in the effective work of Christ Jesus.

The point of all this is that salvation in Christ is not simply a theological truth, predicated on God's prior action and the historical work of Christ. Salvation is an experienced reality, made so by the person of the Spirit coming into our lives. One simply cannot be a Christian in any Pauline sense without the effective work of the Trinity. We will pursue this truth in greater detail in chapter 8 below. For now we offer a few concluding words about the Trinity and its further implications for our present life in Christ.

CONCLUSIONS AND IMPLICATIONS

The upshot of all this is twofold. First, to return to the preceding chapter for a moment, Paul would not recognize the language or the theological assertions of those who consider him to have identified the Spirit with the risen Christ. His assumptions lay elsewhere, with the one God, now bringing salvation through the cooperative work of the three divine Persons: Father, Son, and Spirit. At points where the work of any or all overlaps, Paul's language tends to be flexible—precisely because salvation for him is the activity of the one God.

Salvation is an experienced reality, made so by the person of the Spirit coming into our lives.

Second, one may grant that Paul's trinitarian assumptions and descriptions, which form the basis of the later formulas, never move toward calling the Spirit "God" and never wrestle with the philosophical and theological implications of those assumptions and descriptions. But neither is there evidence that he lacked clarity as to the distinctions between, and the specific roles of, the three divine Persons who accomplished so great salvation for us all.

Moreover, that the Spirit alone knows the mind of God, "the deep things of God," as Paul puts it, and that God knows the mind of the Spirit indicate not only functional trinitarianism, but something close to ontological trinitarianism (having to do with God's very being). So also with the clear evidence of the Spirit's unity with Christ—in receiving a fresh supply of the Spirit, it is the Spirit of Jesus Christ whom Paul receives—yet the clear distinctions between Christ and the Spirit.

But what does such trinitarianism mean for us? Several things. First, it means that the Spirit must be reinstated into the Trinity, where he has never been excluded in our creeds and liturgies, but has been practically excluded from the experienced life of the church. To be a Pauline Christian means to take the Spirit with full seriousness as the way the eternal God is ever present with his people.

Second, God as Trinity, including the Holy Spirit, is the ground of both our unity and our diversity within the believing community. Although we will pursue this point further in chapter 6, suffice it here to say that the Trinity is the ground for the church's much-needed unity. God himself—Father, Son, and Holy Spirit—

is one God; and we are all his one people. The effective agent of our unity, according to Paul in Ephesians 2 and 3 (cf. 1 Cor 12:13), is none other than the Holy Spirit.

But according to 1 Corinthians 12:4–6, the Trinity is also the ground for affirming the church's obvious diversity within its unity. The more truly trinitarian we are in our thinking and experience, the more vigorously we should affirm our diversity and pursue our unity.

The Spirit must be reinstated into the Trinity, where he has never been excluded in our creeds and liturgies, but has been practically excluded from the experienced life of the church.

Finally, although Paul does not press this point, the triune nature of God makes clear that God is essentially a *relational* being. This reality, especially the relationship between the Father and the Son, is one of the special contributions of John in the New Testament. If Paul does not press this reality as explicitly as John does, the offhand mention of the relationship between the Spirit and the Father in 1 Corinthians 2:10–11 and Romans 8:26–27 comes out at the same point. The Spirit, who reveals to us the "deep things of God" (that is, the cross as God's wisdom), does so because he alone knows the mind of God; and the Spirit is our intercessor, who prays through us in keeping with God's own pleasure, precisely because the Spirit and the Father each knows the mind of the other.

This not only gives us confidence in our praying, but should constantly remind us that the one God lives in eternal relationship within himself as the triune God. The relational implications of this for us, both toward God and toward one another, should become a primary part of our paradigm of life in the Spirit as we live together the life of the future in our postmodern world.

NOTES

1. Arius was a bishop in Alexandria who at the beginning of the fourth century argued that "there was a time when Christ was not," thus positing Christ as a divine being, to be sure, but a created one, who was not fully equal with God. It took the Jehovah's Witnesses many decades to discover that they were Arians. Since that day they stopped "witnessing" about "kingdom" issues, as had been their wont, and instead pursued their anti-trinitarian Arianism with full and knowledgeable vigor.

2. And even our term "Person" causes all kinds of difficulties, partly because it stems from a Latin word that does not carry all the baggage that our word does. For example, our word "person" implies self-consciousness, so that "three Persons" should mean three separate and distinct expressions of "self-consciousness," but neither the Greek *hypostasis* nor the Latin *persona* carries such a nuance.

3. The fifth-century ecumenical council at which was drafted the orthodox formulation of the Trinity that still stands today in both the Catholic and Protestant traditions.

4. Pinnock ("Concept," 2): "Modern Christians are largely content to be trinitarian in belief, but binitarian in practice"; he notes that much the same had been said by A. M. Hunter (*Interpreting Paul's Gospel* [London: SCM, 1954] 112) and F. C. Synge ("The Holy Spirit and the Sacraments," *Scottish Journal of Theology* 6 [1953] 65).

5. On this whole question, and especially on Paul as a trinitarian, see the section entitled "What About the Trinity?" by David Ford, in Frances Young and David Ford, *Meaning and Truth in 2 Corinthians* (Grand Rapids: Eerdmans, 1987) 255–60.

6. So also Pinnock, "Concept," 116–18, who likewise notes that the later expression of trinitarian faith grows out of a trinitarian encounter with the one God in his saving work.

7. For a thorough analysis of this text, see *GEP*, 362–65.

8. To return to an issue raised in ch. 3 above, affirmations like this also shut down all possibilities that Paul could ever identify the risen Christ with the Spirit.

9. See *GEP*, 777–84, on Titus 3:5–6. Of all my memories of the Pentecostal tradition in which I was reared (which differs in many significant respects from that of today), I suppose this particular expression of "Pentecostal spirituality" has left its most indelible imprint on my consciousness. Here were people—often poor, and sometimes suffering, people—whose experience of the Spirit in "Spirit baptism" had assured them of God's love and of their own future glory. The gospel songs on which I was raised were the most constant reinforcement of this reality. If to the outsider we seemed to be looking for "pie in the sky" and living as

escapists (cf. Robert Mapes Anderson, *Vision of the Disinherited* [1979; reprint, Peabody, Mass.: Hendrickson, 1992]), in fact we were merely expressing what we believed Paul and his churches also to have experienced—that God loves us despite outward appearances to the contrary. And it was our experience of the Holy Spirit, who poured out this love of God into our hearts, that gave us this certainty.

10. For a complete list of relevant texts (all of which are analyzed in *GEP*), see *GEP*, 48, n. 39.

THE BEGINNING OF THE END—THE SPIRIT AS EVIDENCE OF THE "PRESENCE OF THE FUTURE"

*The visitation of God through the Spirit establishes
believers as a thoroughly eschatological people,
who live the life of the future in the present
as they await the consummation.*

At a recent coffee hour with students in the Regent College atrium, one student asked, "If you were to return to the pastoral ministry, what would you do [meaning, How would you go about it? What would you emphasize?]?" My answer was immediate: "No matter how long it might take, I would set about with a single passion to help a local body of believers recapture the New Testament church's understanding of itself as an eschatological community." I then set about to explain why, and what that might look like in the present day.

I have no illusions that it would be easy, I further explained. The one feature that probably more than any other distances the New Testament church from us is the thoroughgoing *eschatological* perspective from which believers viewed everything that God had wrought through Christ and the Spirit.

Eschatology has to do with the time of the End, and refers first of all to Jewish expectations that God through his Messiah would bring a dramatic end to the "present age." This in turn would be followed by the "coming age," signaled by the resurrection of the dead and the gift of the promised Holy Spirit. These expectations may be diagrammed as in figure 1.

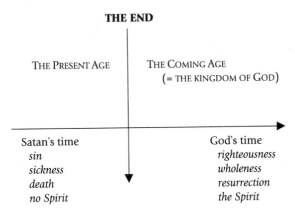

Figure 1.

A unique twist to this end-time expectation conditioned the earliest Christians' existence in every way; and the outpoured Spirit was essential to this new understanding. The first Christians believed that the fulfillment of God's Old Testament covenant promises had begun with the work of Christ and their experience of the promised Spirit. In their view they were already living in the beginning of the end times. Their new perspective, which conditioned everything about them, may be sketched as in figure 2.

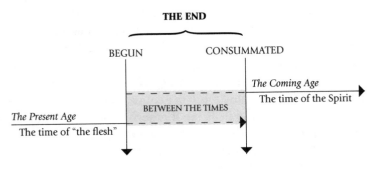

Figure 2.

The first clue to this outlook came from Jesus' own proclamation of the kingdom—as a present reality in his ministry, although still a future event. But it was the resurrection of Christ and the gift of the promised Spirit that completely altered the primitive church's perspective, both about Jesus and about the people of God. In place of the totally future, still-to-come endtime expectation of their Jewish roots, with its hope of a coming Messiah accompanied by the resurrection of the dead, the early believers recognized that the future had already been set in motion. The resurrection of Christ marked the beginning of the End, the turning of the ages.

However, the End had only begun; they still awaited the final event, the (now second) coming of their Messiah Jesus, at which time they too would experience the resurrection/transformation of the body. They lived "between the times"; *already* the future had begun, *not yet* had it been completely fulfilled. This already/not yet perspective, in which they believed themselves already to be living in the time of the End, even though it was yet to be consummated, is the eschatological framework that determines everything about them—how they lived, how they thought, and how they understood their own place in the present world, which was now understood to be on its way out.

PAUL'S END-TIME PERSPECTIVE

This new perspective about the end times[1] absolutely determines Paul's theological outlook—how he thinks and talks about Christ, salvation, the church, ethics, the present, the future, everything. This is reflected both in his explicit language and in a whole variety of presuppositional ways. "We are those," he reminds the Corinthians, "upon whom the ends of the ages *have come*" (1 Cor 10:11). On another occasion, he tells them Christ's death and resurrection have already passed sentence on the present age (2 Cor 5:14–15), which is thus "passing away" (1 Cor 7:31). With the coming of Christ the new order has begun; all things have become new (2 Cor 5:17). It is no longer an option to view things from the perspective of the "flesh," that is, from the "old order" point of view. The death and resurrection of Christ and the gift of the Spirit mean both death to the old and a radical, newly constituted life in the present.

For Paul, therefore, salvation in Christ is a fundamentally eschatological reality, meaning first of all that God's final salvation of his people has already been accomplished by Christ. In a sort of divine time warp, the future condemnation that we all richly deserve has been transferred from the future into the past, having been borne by Christ (Rom 8:1–3). Thus we "have been saved" (Eph 2:8). Since our final salvation has not yet been fully realized, he can likewise speak of salvation as something presently in process ("we are being saved," 1 Cor 1:18) and as yet to be completed ("we shall be saved," Rom 5:9). "Redemption" is both "already" (Eph 1:7) and "not yet" (Eph 4:30), as is our "adoption" (Rom 8:15 and 23) and "justification" (= the gift of righteousness; Rom 5:1 and Gal 5:5).

This essential framework likewise causes Paul to see the church as an end-time community, whose members live in the present as those stamped with eternity. We live as strangers on earth; our true citizenship is in heaven (Phil 3:20). Ethical life, therefore, does not consist of rules to live by. Rather, empowered by the Spirit, we now live the life of the future in the present age, the life that characterizes God himself. This is why, for example, Paul appeals to end-time realities as the reason believers may not resolve present grievances before pagan courts (1 Cor 6:1–4). Their heavenly citizenship trivializes such grievances—and puts believers in the awkward position of asking for a ruling by the very people that they themselves will eventually judge.[2] Believers have tasted of the life to come; and the full and final realization of the future is so certain that God's new people become heavenly radicals as they live in the "already" but "not yet" of the present age.

Since this eschatological perspective so thoroughly conditions Paul's outlook on everything, our first task is to look at the crucial role the Spirit plays in "salvation in Christ." We will then point out how this understanding of the Spirit affects the central passion of Paul's life, the inclusion of the Gentiles in the end-time people of God.

THE SPIRIT AS THE EVIDENCE AND GUARANTEE OF THE FUTURE

Paul derived his already/not yet eschatological perspective from two experiences at the beginning of his life in Christ: his encounter with the risen Christ on the Damascus Road ("I have seen the Lord," he tells the Corinthians), and the subsequent gift of the Spirit. In Paul's pre-Christian understanding, the resurrection of the dead and the gift of the Spirit were the two primary events that marked the end of the ages. Both of these have now been set in motion.

First, from his Jewish roots Paul understood the resurrection of the dead to be the final event on God's earthly calendar, the unmistakable evidence for the full arrival of the End.[3] For Paul *the* resurrection has already taken place when Christ was raised from the dead, thus initiating the final doom of death and thereby guaranteeing our resurrection. Christ's resurrection makes ours both inevitable and necessary—inevitable, because his is the firstfruits that sets the whole process in motion; necessary, because death is God's enemy as well as ours, and our resurrection spells the end to the final enemy of the living God, who gives life to all who live (1 Cor 15:20–28). Believers therefore live between the times with regard to the two resurrections. We have *already* been "raised with Christ," which guarantees our *future* bodily resurrection (Rom 6:4–5; 8:10–11).

Ethical life does not consist of rules to live by.

Second, the gift of the Spirit is the crowning evidence that God's end-time promises are being fulfilled. For Paul, neither his own experience of the Spirit nor his perception of that experience makes sense apart from the perspective of the fulfilled promise and salvation as already but not yet. From his Jewish heritage he well understood that the Spirit was part of the promise for the future. As noted in chapter 2 above, Jeremiah and Ezekiel gave an eschatological cast to the promises of the new covenant. This perspective became thoroughgoing in later Jewish expectations on the basis of Joel 2:28-30, that "afterward I will pour out my Spirit on all people."

This is why the Spirit is crucial to Paul's understanding of Christian existence. The gift of the outpoured Spirit meant that the messianic age had already arrived. The Spirit is thus the central element in this altered perspective,[4] the key to which is Paul's firm conviction that the Spirit was both the certain evidence that the future had dawned, and the absolute guarantee of its final consummation.

The Spirit as Down Payment, Firstfruits, and Seal

This twofold role of the Spirit (as both evidence and guarantee of the future) emerges in a variety of ways throughout Paul's letters, but nowhere more prominently than in three metaphors for the Spirit that are unique to him: down payment, firstfruits, and seal. All three images are apt; each may emphasize the Spirit either as the present evidence of future realities or as the assurance of the final glory, or both of these simultaneously.

1. The metaphor of "down payment," which occurs three times (2 Cor 1:21-22; 5:5; Eph 1:14), appears exclusively in Paul in the New Testament; and he uses it exclusively to refer to the Spirit. The word shows up often in Greek commercial papyri as a technical term for the first installment (hence "down payment") of a total amount due.[5] As such, it both establishes the contractual obligation and guarantees its fulfillment. For Paul it thus serves in all three instances to emphasize both the already and the not yet of our present existence.[6]

This is especially clear in Ephesians 1:14, where Paul calls the "promised" Holy Spirit the "down payment on our inheritance." One can scarcely miss the "already/not yet" presuppositions of this language. On the one hand, the "Holy Spirit of the promise" and "our inheritance" come directly out of the future expectations of Paul's Jewish heritage: the Spirit whom we have received is the fulfillment of the promise. On the other hand, this "fulfilled promise" is likewise the guarantee of our future inheritance. The Spirit, therefore, serves as God's down payment in our present lives, the certain evidence that the future has come into the present, and the sure guarantee that the future will be realized in full measure.

2. The metaphor of "firstfruits," used of the Spirit in Romans 8:23, demonstrates equally well the Spirit's role in Paul's changed eschatological perspective. This metaphor, used previously of Christ's resurrection as the guarantee of ours (1 Cor 15:20, 23), reflects in a special way the tension of present existence as already/ not yet *and* the guarantee of our certain future. The larger context of Romans 8:14–30 is especially noteworthy. With the Spirit playing the leading role, Paul in vv. 15–17 has struck the dual themes of our present position as children (who are thus joint heirs with Christ of the Father's glory) and of our present existence as one of weakness and suffering as we await that glory. These are the two themes taken up in vv. 18–27. By the Spirit we have already received our adoption as God's children, but what is already is also not yet. Therefore, by the same Spirit who functions for us as firstfruits, we await our final adoption, in the form of the redemption of our bodies. The first sheaf of grain is God's pledge to us of the final harvest. Thus, in one of Paul's clearest passages outlining his basic eschatological framework, the Spirit plays the key role in our present existence, as both evidence and guarantee that the future is now and yet to be.

3. The third metaphor, "seal," also occurs three times with direct reference to the Spirit (2 Cor 1:21–22; Eph 1:13; 4:30). In literal usage a seal referred to a stamped impression in wax or clay, signaling ownership and authenticity, and carrying with it the protection of the owner. In Paul, as Ephesians 1:13 and 4:30 make certain, the seal is a metaphor for the Spirit, by whom God has marked believers and claimed them as his own.

In contrast to "down payment," there is nothing essentially eschatological in this image; nonetheless, Paul's metaphor plainly carries such overtones, emphasizing either the present or the future. In 2 Corinthians 1:21–22, the gift of the eschatological Spirit in the lives of the Corinthians serves as the seal that both marks them off as God's possession and authenticates Paul's apostleship among them. Likewise, in Ephesians 1:13, by sealing them with the Holy Spirit, God stamped the Gentile recipients of that letter as his own possession. At the same time, the guarantee of the future in the metaphor is expressly stated in Ephesians 4:30 ("with whom you were sealed *for the day of redemption*").

These metaphors serve as starting points for us to penetrate Paul's understanding. The Spirit is the evidence that the eschatological promises of Paul's Jewish heritage have been fulfilled. At the same time, the Spirit as God's empowering presence enables the people of God not simply to endure the present as they await the final consummation, but to do so with verve (with "spirit," if you will). And that is because the future is as sure as the presence of the Spirit is an experienced reality; hence the significance of the dynamic and experiential nature of the Spirit's coming into the life of the believer and the church.

> *The Spirit is the evidence that the eschatological promises of Paul's Jewish heritage have been fulfilled.*

The Spirit and Resurrection

The most prominent feature of what is "not yet" in Pauline eschatology is the bodily resurrection of believers. Here again is a place in Paul's understanding where the Spirit plays a decisive role. But that role is not, as is sometimes asserted, that of agency;[7] rather the indwelling Spirit serves as the divine pledge of our future bodily resurrection. That is, the Spirit does not *bring about* our resurrection, but *guarantees* it. Moreover, since the final resurrection takes place in the sphere characterized above all by the Spirit's presence, Paul sees the closest kind of connection between the Spirit and the nature of the resurrection body. A few words about each of these matters are warranted.

First, resurrection, both Christ's and ours, is invariably expressed in terms of God's activity, attributed at times to God's power.[8] The clearest expression of the Spirit's role in this reality is Romans 8:11. Here Paul does not say, as some have read it, "If the Spirit who raised Christ dwells in you." Rather he says, "If the Spirit *of him [God]* who raised Christ dwells in you." Paul's point is that if the Spirit dwells in us, that is, the Spirit of the very God who raised Christ, then that says something significant about our own future—that the presence in our lives of the Spirit of the God who raised Christ guarantees the "future life" of our mortal bodies as well, destined for death though they still be (v. 10).

To this clause Paul adds a prepositional phrase, which ended up in the textual history of Romans in two different forms. One, taken up by the NIV and others, reads, "through the Spirit who dwells in you." Although this reading speaks clearly of agency, it is patently secondary.[9] Both the manuscript evidence and the primary rule of textual criticism (namely, the reading that best explains how the other came about is the original) support the text that reads, "*because of* the Spirit who dwells in you."

Paul's point is simply that we can be certain that our bodies, though destined for death, will be given life, precisely *because* of the Spirit who indwells us. Thus, in this passage, as in all others that speak to the question, the Spirit guarantees our future, including our bodily resurrection.

The Spirit does not bring about our resurrection, but guarantees it.

That is also the clear sense of the metaphor "down payment" in 2 Corinthians 5:5 and the metaphor "firstfruits" in Romans 8:23. In each case the metaphors signal the Spirit's presence in our lives as the sure guarantee that we shall realize our final "adoption, the redemption of our bodies." Thus, even though one could hardly object to the Spirit's agency with regard to this final realization of the future, Paul's point is a consistently different one, namely, that the Spirit is both the evidence and the guarantee of the future, including the final expression of the future.

That leads, second, to a word about the nature of our redeemed bodies, since in 1 Corinthians 15:44–48 Paul insists on calling them "spiritual bodies." This expression does not refer to their substance, as though Paul intended to compare them with our present bodies composed of material substance.[10] Rather, he is contrasting our present existence with our heavenly one; the future body is supernaturally fitted for the final life of the Spirit, totally unhindered by any of its present weaknesses.

Left to his own, and apart from the language dictated by his opponents in Corinth, Paul later speaks of the two modes of our bodily existence as "the body of our [present] humiliation" that God will transform into the likeness of "the body of Christ's [present] glory" (Phil 3:21). The "body of glory" is his "Spiritual body," the body supernaturally transformed for existence in the final realm of the Spirit. Thus, the "redemption of the body" has to do with the present body's becoming a "Spiritual body," in that it will be totally transformed, fully adapted, for the life that is to be, of which the Spirit's presence now is the guarantee.

We note finally in this regard that Paul's worldview is not tinged by Greek body/spirit dualism. The Greeks considered the body a second-rate shell for the spirit, despised and subdued in the present and finally sloughed off as believers attain true spirituality. This was apparently the Corinthians' position, and Paul attacks it twice in his letters to them.

For them the Spirit meant present ecstasy, life above and beyond mere bodily weaknesses, and thus evidence of being released finally from bodily existence altogether. For Paul the Spirit meant empowering for life in the midst of present bodily weaknesses—in a body obviously in the process of decay. Thus in 2 Corinthians 5:5 he reaffirms his position from 1 Corinthians 15:35–58 that the presence of the Spirit means that these "decaying bodies" have also been stamped with eternity; they are destined for resurrection and hence transformation into the likeness of Christ's now glorified body. God, Paul argues, "has fashioned us for this." The Spirit, whom the Corinthians have come to understand in a triumphalistic way (that is, as carrying them somehow above the trials and troubles of earthly life), is rather the guarantee, the down payment from God, that these bodies are also destined for a "Spiritual" (= glorified) future.

The point of this passage, I should add, needs to be heard again and again over against every encroachment of Hellenistic dualism that would negate the body in favor of the soul. God made us whole people; and in Christ he has redeemed us wholly. In the Christian view there is no dichotomy between body and spirit that either indulges the body because it is irrelevant or punishes it to purify the spirit.

This pagan view of physical existence insinuates itself into Christian theology in a number of subtle ways, including the penchant on the part of some to "save souls" while caring little for people's material needs. Not the immortality of the soul but the resurrection of the body is the Christian creed, based on New Testament revelation. That creed does not lead to crass materialism; rather it affirms a holistic view of redemption, which is predicated in part on the doctrine of creation—both the physical and spiritual orders are good because God created them—and in part on the doctrine of redemption, including the consummation—the whole fallen order, including the body, has been redeemed in Christ and awaits its final redemption. The clear evidence that the body is included in final redemption is the presence of the Spirit, which does not move us toward a false, Hellenistic spirituality, but toward the biblical view noted here.

THE SPIRIT AND THE MISSION TO THE GENTILES

Partly in preparation for the next chapter, we need finally to note the role of the Spirit in the heart of Paul's own calling and mission—the promised inclusion of the Gentiles in the end-time people of God. This was the singular passion of his life; and their inclusion together with Jews as one people of God on the basis of the work of Christ and the gift of the Spirit, and therefore apart from Jewish Torah observance, is what drives the argument of both Galatians and Romans and is the presupposition of the argument of Ephesians. This comes out most clearly in Romans, whose principal concern comes to its climax in 15:5–13, at the conclusion of the theological argument of the letter. It is as Jews and Gentiles together "with one mouth . . . glorify the God and Father of our Lord Jesus Christ" that the eschatological promises of God regarding the inclusion of the Gentiles, expressed in the final series of Old Testament texts in vv. 9–12, find their fulfillment. The role of the Spirit in this fulfillment is a staple in the argument of Romans. It is expressly stated elsewhere in two key passages.

The most significant passage in this regard is Galatians 3:14, since the promise of the Spirit is equated with the blessing of Abraham, even though the Old Testament passage does not mention the Spirit. Since the "blessing of Abraham" came in the form of a "promise," this word is the one Paul uses throughout the argument of Galatians 3 to refer to the blessing of the Abrahamic covenant. In a statement crucial to this argument, Paul says the fulfillment of this promised blessing for the Gentiles is in their having experienced the Spirit as a living and dynamic reality. The blessing of Abraham, therefore, is not simply "justification by faith." Rather, it refers to the life of the future now available to Jew and Gentile alike, achieved through the death of Christ but applied through the dynamic ministry of the Spirit—and all of this by faith.

Likewise in Ephesians 1:13-14, addressing his Gentile readers directly, Paul assures them that they, too, have been sealed by God as his possession, by giving them "the Holy Spirit of the promise" (= the Holy Spirit promised to Israel). By that same token God also guaranteed the final inheritance for Jew and Gentile alike, since the Spirit is God's down payment of our (Jew and Gentile together) inheritance. Thus, with a subtle shift of pronouns Paul moves from "our" (= Jews) having obtained the inheritance, to "your" (= Gentiles) having been sealed by the "promised Holy Spirit," to the Spirit as God's down payment on "our" (= Jew and Gentile together) final inheritance.

This is eschatological language. The Spirit as the fulfilled promise confirms that God's future salvation has now come. Jew and Gentile together have obtained the inheritance, which they also patiently await. "A person is not a Jew 'outwardly,' " Paul says in another place (Rom 2:29), nor is true circumcision (that which identifies God's people) a matter of cutting off the foreskin but is rather "by the Spirit, not by the letter." This, too, for Paul has to do with eschatological fulfillment, this time of Deuteronomy 30:1-6, with its promise of a renewed people whose hearts God has circumcised.

So also with the language of hope. In Ephesians 4:1-3, Paul's concern is that his readers "maintain the unity [of Jew and Gentile as one people of God] effected by the Spirit." The one body, he adds in v. 4, formed by the one Spirit, also lives in one hope of their calling, precisely because through the Spirit Gentiles have become fellow heirs with Jews of the final inheritance (1:13–14). And in Romans 15:13, having noted that Christ is the fulfillment of Isaiah 11:10—he is the one in whom the Gentiles now hope—Paul concludes by praying that his predominantly Gentile readers will "abound in [this] hope by the power of the Spirit." Thus the Spirit for Paul is the key to the *present fulfillment* of the *eschatological* inclusion of the Gentiles in the people of God.

> *The Spirit is the key to the future orientation of Paul and the early church.*

In light of all this evidence, including that already given in chapter 2, it is fair to conclude that the Spirit is the key to the future orientation of Paul and the early church. By the Spirit's presence believers have tasted of the life to come and are now oriented toward its consummation. "We are saved in hope," Paul tells the Romans (8:24); by the power of the Spirit we "abound in hope" (Rom 15:13). And for the early Christians "hope" was a content word; that is, it did not mean mere wishfulness but absolute certainty.

Despite what is often implied to the contrary, however, Paul's primary emphasis is not on this certain and eagerly awaited future that the Spirit guarantees. It is rather on the Spirit as the demonstration that the future has already been set in motion. This is especially true at the very heart of matters for him, that through Christ and the Spirit, God is already calling out a people for his name, who will live the life of the future in their present existence together as they await the consummation.

NOTES

1. On this question, the classic is G. Vos, *The Pauline Eschatology* (1930; reprint, Grand Rapids: Baker, 1979]), esp. pp. 1–61, a book that was years ahead of its time.

2. For a full discussion of this text and the eschatological framework that conditions Paul's response, see Fee, *The First Epistle to the Corinthians* (NICNT; Grand Rapids: Eerdmans, 1987) 228–48.

3. That Paul never lost this perspective is witnessed most vividly in 1 Cor 15:20–28. When Christ raises the believing dead, that spells the death of death itself; thus Christ turns over all things to the Father, who is all and in all. See Fee, *1 Corinthians*, 746–60.

4. F. F. Bruce (*The Epistle to the Galatians* [NIGTC; Grand Rapids: Eerdmans, 1982] 232) rightly calls this "the most distinctive feature in Paul's doctrine of the Spirit."

5. See J. H. Moulton and G. Milligan, *The Vocabulary of the Greek Testament Illustrated from the Papyri and Other Non-Literary Sources* (London: Hodder and Stoughton, 1914–30) 79; cf. the discussion on 2 Cor 1:21–22 in *GEP*, 287–96.

6. So much is this so, that the NIV translates *arrabōn* in both 2 Corinthians passages as "a deposit, guaranteeing what is to come." That is an accurate English translation of the *idea* (as opposed to a merely literal translation), although the phrase "guaranteeing what is to come" is only inherent in the metaphor itself—it does not occur in Paul's own sentence as such.

7. Although there is nothing inherently difficult theologically with this assertion, and indeed it may very well be so, nonetheless one cannot derive such a view from anything Paul says explicitly. For the contrary view, and the arguments against it, see *GEP*, 553–54 and 808–10.

8. See 1 Thess 1:10; 1 Cor 6:14; 15:15; 2 Cor 4:14; 13:4; Gal 1:1; Rom 4:24; 6:4; 8:11; 10:9; Col 2:12; Eph 1:20; plus the texts where Christ's resurrection is expressed in the "divine passive" (1 Thess 4:14; 1 Cor 15:12, 20; 2 Cor 5:15; Rom 4:25; 6:9; 7:4; 8:34).

9. On this question see esp. *GEP*, 543, n. 205, and 552, n. 231, on Rom 8:10–11.

10. For the exegetical support of what is said here, see *GEP*, 263–71.

A PEOPLE FOR HIS NAME—THE SPIRIT AND THE PEOPLE OF GOD

*Based on the work of Christ, the Spirit calls forth
a newly constituted people and makes
them "a people for his name."*

A single person is sitting at home in front of the TV; a Christian broadcast is on, a sermon is preached, an invitation is given, and the person responds by "accepting Christ." But the only "church" the person attends is by way of the TV, with no connection to a local body of believers. The question: Is this person saved? I would answer: Only God knows; but such salvation lies totally outside the New Testament frame of reference.[1]

One of the sure members of the modern world's "trinity," along with relativism and secularism, is individualism. Recapturing the biblical sense of the significance of the individual, but revising it to fit a nonbiblical, naturalistic worldview, the Enlightenment led the modern Western world into a totally individualistic understanding of life, which has never been more prevalent than it is today. The individual is the be-all and end-all of everything; subservience of individual rights to the common good has become the new "heresy" to be rejected at all costs. The individual is god; narcissistic self-interest and self-centeredness is the chief end of life.

Unfortunately, in recognizing the biblical emphasis on the significance of the individual, North American Christianity in particular has also tended to buy into our cultural version of this emphasis. So much is this so that any hint of a return to the biblical emphasis on the people of God as a community of believers is often seen as a threat to our significance as individuals. Paul's view is considerably different.

We have already noted that Paul's understanding of salvation in Christ has both continuity and discontinuity with Paul's Jewish heritage. Continuity, the concern of this chapter, resides in God's still "saving a people for his name,"[2] a people who fulfill the covenant with Abraham (Gen 12:2–3). Discontinuity, the concern of the next chapter, lies in the fact that the people of God are no longer so on the basis of "nation," but on the basis of individual entry through faith in Christ Jesus and the gift of the Spirit, signaled by baptism.[3]

Paul can hardly help himself: his focus and concern are always on the people as a whole. Though entered individually, salvation is seldom if ever thought of simply as a one-on-one relationship with God. While such a relationship is included, to be sure, "to be saved" means especially to be joined to the people of God. In this sense, the third-century church father Cyprian had it right: there is no salvation outside the church, because God is saving *a people* for his name, not a miscellaneous, unconnected set of individuals. Thus our present concern is with the primary goal of salvation: an eschatological people, who together live the life of the future in the present age as they await the final consummation.

PAUL AND THE PEOPLE OF GOD

Paul's most common form of address to the recipients of his letters is "the saints." This does not mean they are exceptional Christians, either in the sense of "St. Patrick" or "St. Theresa" or that of "my Aunt Betty is a real saint." He is simply referring to all the people of God in a given city or region. By this designation Paul deliberately uses a term for God's people from his Jewish heritage. The term "saints" refers to God's "holy people"—chosen, redeemed, and now gathered before God at Sinai to fulfill his own purposes in the world (Exod 19:5-6). The term is used again in the eschatological vision of Daniel 7:18 for "the saints of the Most High" who "will receive the kingdom and will possess it forever." This vision Paul sees as fulfilled through Christ and the Spirit.

All of the language Paul uses to refer to the newly formed people of God thus derives from the Old Testament. They are God's "people,"[4] because they are God's "elect."[5] Those who live by the rule of "neither circumcision nor uncircumcision," and only those, are the "Israel of God" (Gal 6:16). The most common designation is "the church" *(ekklēsia)*, which Paul borrows from the Septuagint, which regularly uses *ekklēsia* to translate the Hebrew *qāhāl*, referring most often to the "congregation of Israel." This abundant use of Old Testament "people" language makes clear that Paul saw the church not only as in continuity with the old covenant people of God, but as in the true succession of that people.

One of the essential features of this continuity is the corporate nature of God's people. God chose, and made a covenant with, not individual Israelites but a people who would bear God's name and be for God's purposes. Although individual Israelites could forfeit their position in Israel, this never affected God's design or purposes with the people as his people. This is true even when the majority failed, and the people were reduced to a "remnant." That remnant was still Israel—loved, chosen, and redeemed by God.

This is the consistent viewpoint of Paul as well. Although entered individually, the church as a whole is the object of God's saving activity in Christ. God is choosing and saving a people for his name.

Perhaps nothing illustrates this point as vividly as two passages in 1 Corinthians (5:1-13; 6:1-11), where Paul speaks to rather flagrant sins of particular individuals. In both cases Paul aims his heaviest artillery not at the individual sinners but at the church for its failure to deal with these matters. In 5:1-13 the man is not even spoken to—he is simply to be put out—and his partner is not mentioned at all. Everything is directed at the church—for its arrogance on the one hand, and for its failure to act on the other.

So also in 6:1-11. In this case Paul does finally speak to the plaintiff (vv. 7-8a) and to the defendant (vv. 8b-11), but only after he has scored the church for allowing such a thing to happen at all among God's eschatological community and then for failing to act. What is obviously at stake in these cases is the church itself, and its role as God's redeemed and redemptive alternative to Corinth.

This concern for God's saving a people for his glory is further demonstrated by the frequency of one of the most common, but frequently overlooked, words in Paul's ethical exhortations: *allēlōn* ("one another/each other"). *Everything* is done *allēlōn*. They are members of one another (Rom 12:5; Eph 4:25), who are to build up one another (1 Thess 5:11; Rom 14:19), to care for one another (1 Cor 12:25), to love one another (1 Thess 3:12; 4:9; 2 Thess 1:3; Rom 13:8), to pursue one another's good (1 Thess 5:15), to bear with one another in love (Eph 4:2); to bear one another's burdens (Gal 6:2); to be kind and compassionate to one another, forgiving one another (Eph 4:32; cf. Col 3:13), to submit to one another (Eph 5:21), to consider one another better than ourselves (Phil 2:3; cf. Rom 12:10), to be devoted to one another in love (Rom 12:10), to live in harmony with one another (Rom 12:16).

God is not just saving individuals and preparing them for heaven; rather, he is creating *a people* among whom he can live and who in their life together will reproduce God's life and character. This view of salvation is consistent throughout Paul's letters. It is demonstrated most clearly in his references to the Spirit, who plays the key role not only in forming the people of God, but also in their life together and in their worship.

THE SPIRIT AND THE BELIEVING COMMUNITY

We will note in the next chapters that the transforming, renewing work of the Spirit begins the individual's life in Christ; the same is true of the believing community. The community of God's people owe their life together as a body to their common, lavish experience of the Spirit. The question Paul answers in 1 Corinthians 12:13 is not how people become believers—although that is obviously involved—but how the many of them, composed of

Jew and Gentile, slave and free, make up the one body of Christ. Paul's answer: All alike were immersed in the same reality, Spirit, and all alike were caused to drink to the fill of the same reality, Spirit, so as to form one body in Christ.

Likewise, in 2 Corinthians 3:1–3, Paul describes the believing community as "his letter of recommendation," having become so because they were "written by the Spirit," as it were. Again, although Paul uses different imagery, he makes the point that the Spirit is responsible for their having together become God's people in Corinth.

The community of God's people owe their life together as a body to their common, lavish experience of the Spirit.

Created and formed *by* the Spirit, the early communities thus became a fellowship *of* the Spirit. The concept of koinōnia ("fellowship") is a broad one in Paul. It begins as fellowship with God through Christ (1 Cor 1:9), which in turn brings believers into fellowship with one another. In the trinitarian benediction of 2 Corinthians 13:14, Paul chooses koinōnia to describe the ministry of the Spirit. Although this term refers chiefly to "a participation in the Spirit himself," such participation is common to them all and thus also includes the "fellowship" created and sustained by the Spirit. So also in Philippians 2:1–4, part of the basis of his appeal to unity and harmony in v. 1 is their common participation (both Paul's and theirs together) in the Spirit (cf. 1:27, "stand firm in one Spirit"). Likewise, common love brought about by the Spirit serves as the basis of an appeal to the Roman believers to support him with their prayers (Rom 15:30; cf. Col 1:8).

For Paul the fact that both Jews and Gentiles are included in God's family is the most remarkable aspect of this newly formed fellowship. In Christ's death God has triumphed over the former prejudices on both sides (Eph 2:14–18). Paul's sense of wonder at this shines throughout Ephesians. Thus 1:13–14 is not first of all about individual conversions; rather, Paul is rejoicing because Gentiles ("you also") have been included in Christ along with Jews as God's inheritance. This has been certified by the remarkable reality that they were given the promised Holy Spirit as seal and down payment of that inheritance.

This Spirit-forged unity is also the point of Ephesians 2:18. Just as Christ's death made the "one body" a possibility by abolishing what divided Jew and Gentile, so now through Christ both "have access to the Father *in one Spirit.*" Jews and Gentiles have been formed by the Spirit into one body (cf. 4:4), and as they dwell together in the one Spirit they have common access as one people into the presence of God.

PAUL'S IMAGES FOR THE COMMUNITY OF THE SPIRIT

The centrality of the Spirit to Paul's view of the believing community emerges especially in his three major images for the church (family, temple, body); the first two of these also reflect continuity with the Old Testament.

God's Family

This image, which occurs explicitly only twice (Eph 2:19; 1 Tim 3:15; cf. 2 Cor 6:18), flows naturally out of Paul's reference to God as Father, believers as brothers and sisters, and the apostle as a household manager (see 1 Cor 4:1-2). The imagery itself receives no elaboration. What is significant is the role of the Spirit, as both responsible for and evidence of believers' becoming members of God's family.

The imagery first appears in Galatians 4:4-6, where Paul contrasts living under law with the life of faith, life in the Spirit. Living under law is like being a son before he has come of age; he may technically own the whole estate, but he is still no better off than a slave. So with believers, who are no longer under slavery (including slavery to the "powers"); rather they are "sons"[6] with full rights, the evidence of which is their experience of the Spirit, especially the Spirit's cry from within them of "*Abba,* Father."[7]

The primary evidence that we are God's "sons" is that the Spirit within us cries out in the very language of Jesus, the Son. This emphasis is heightened in the Romans parallel, where our ongoing recognition of our "sonship" is the result of "the Spirit himself bearing witness with our spirits that we are the children of God." To which Paul adds, "and if children, then heirs; heirs of God, and fellow heirs with Christ." The repeated use of *adelphoi* ("brothers and sisters") in Paul and the rest of the New Testament to refer to "the saints" is also best explained on the basis of this Spirit-inspired cry to God in the language of Jesus.

God's Temple

On this image, which four times refers to the church,[8] see the discussion in chapter 2 above. It is particularly well suited to the Spirit, since it derives from the sanctuary *(naos)* in Jerusalem, the earthly dwelling of the living God. The Spirit among God's newly formed people means that God has taken up his dwelling in the gathered community. The temple is formed *by* the Spirit; it is thus a habitation *of* the Spirit. Even though Paul transfers this imagery to the individual believer in 1 Corinthians 6:19, its repeated use for the community of believers indicates Paul's primary emphasis.

Christ's Body

With this imagery, which occurs several times in his letters,[9] Paul essentially makes two points: the need for unity *and* for diversity in the believing community, both of which are the work of "the one and the same Spirit" (1 Cor 12:11).

First, the imagery presupposes and argues for the *unity* of the people of God. That is the clear point of Ephesians 4. The church, composed of both Jew and Gentile, forms one body (Eph 2:16). The urgency of the appeal that begins with 4:1 and carries through to the end is that they "keep the unity that the Spirit has given them" (4:3). The basis for the appeal is God the Trinity as expressed in vv. 4–6, which begin by placing the one body in the closest kind of association with the one Spirit. Furthermore, all the sins listed in vv. 25–31 are sins of discord. By giving in to sin, they grieve the Holy Spirit (v. 30), who has formed them into a body and whose continuing presence is intended to bring the body to full maturity. Hence they need to "keep filled with the Spirit" (5:18), to ensure proper worship (vv. 19–20) and proper relationships (5:21–6:9).

Although Paul's larger concern differs in 1 Corinthians 12:12–26, he still emphasizes the Corinthians' unity in the Spirit. The earlier use of "body" imagery in 10:16–17 and 11:29, with reference to the bread of the Lord's Table, had focused on their need for unity. When the imagery recurs in 12:12, unity and diversity are equally stressed. With two sentences (vv. 13 and 14) that begin with the same applicational signal ("for indeed"), Paul argues first that the many of them (Jew, Gentile, slave, free) are one body because of their common lavish experience of Spirit (v. 13). Following v. 14 and its application (vv. 15–20), both of which stress the diverse nature of the body, Paul urges in the second application (vv. 21–26) that there be no "division" among them. This especially recalls the various divisions mentioned throughout the letter. The Spirit has made them *one* body; true Spirituality will maintain that unity, whatever else.

Homogeneous churches lie totally outside Paul's frame of reference.

Likewise in Philippi, where some bickering and posturing were going on that could lead to disunity, Paul urges his readers, especially in light of their struggle against pagan opponents, to "stand firm in the one Spirit" (1:27). This appeal is made on the basis of their common (his and theirs) participation in the Spirit (2:1).

Unity in the body means that believers "walk by the Spirit" so as not to "eat and devour one another" (Gal 3:15–16); it also requires heterogeneous people to submit their diversity to the unifying work of the Spirit. Homogeneous churches lie totally outside Paul's frame of reference. After all, such churches cannot maintain the unity of the Spirit that either Ephesians 2 and 4 or 1 Corinthians 12 call for. God by his Spirit has formed into one body a radically new eschatological fellowship that transcends both race (Jew and Gentile) and socioeconomic status (slave and free).

Second, the Spirit is also responsible for maintaining a necessary and healthy *diversity* in the church. This is the basic concern of the argument in 1 Corinthians 12. The Corinthians' extraordinary and imbalanced emphasis on tongues as the evidence of a fully developed spirituality requires *theological* correction (chs. 12 and 13) before the specific abuse is corrected (ch. 14). Thus every paragraph in chapter 12 except for vv. 21–26 has this theme— the need for diversity in order for the community to be built up. The triune God himself illustrates—and serves as the basis for—this diversity-in-unity (vv. 4–6); and the Spirit in particular is responsible for its being shown forth among them, especially in the many manifestations of his presence "given to each one for the common good" (vv. 7–11). A body cannot be only one part (v. 14); that would be a monstrosity (vv. 15–20). The Spirit who is responsible for their being one body is also the basis for the many parts necessary for the body to function at all.

> *The Spirit is also responsible for maintaining a necessary and healthy diversity in the church.*

Significantly, the body imagery in Ephesians, with its concern for unity, focuses primarily on *relationships* within the church. In 1 Corinthians 12, however, the focus is mainly on the church as a *community gathered for worship,* which is true also of the temple imagery in 3:16–17. This difference in focus is due to the respective errors that were taking place within the gathered community. The early believers did not have buildings called "churches"; they did not "go to church." They *were* the church, and at appointed times and places they assembled *as* the church (1 Cor 11:18). As God's temple, inhabited by his Spirit, they formed a powerful fellowship, marked by works of the Spirit (1 Cor 12:7), including miracles (Gal 3:5) and prophetic utterances (1 Thess 5:19–20; 1 Cor 14:24–25; outsiders exclaim, "surely God is *among you*"). This emphasis on the gathered community serves as the essential background to Paul's understanding of *charismata* ("gracious gifts"), especially in 1 Corinthians 12–14. We will explore these in more detail in chapters 13 and 14 below.

In sum: "to be saved" in the Pauline view means to become part of the *people* of God, who by the Spirit are born into God's *family* and therefore joined to one another as one *body*, whose gatherings in the Spirit form them into God's *temple*. God is not simply saving diverse individuals and preparing them for heaven; rather he is creating *a people* for his name, among whom God can dwell and who in their life *together* will reproduce God's life and character in all its unity and diversity. How the people will live together and what they will look like is taken up in chapters 9 and 10 below.

Before that, we need to look at how "the saints" are now formed. What is new for Paul, and for the rest, is that the people of God are newly constituted by Christ and the Spirit; we enter that people one at a time. Such entry is, above everything else, also the work of the Spirit.

NOTES

1. I get a lot of flack for this view, especially from some in my "revivalist" heritage, and am quoted such texts as Rom 10:9, "that if you confess with your mouth that Jesus is Lord and believe in your heart that God has raised him from the dead, you will be saved." This text, however, presupposes the Christian community as the place where such confession occurs, at the very least at baptism. The earliest Christians would not have understood a believer whose salvation has not been completed by baptism, which includes identification with both Christ and his people.

2. This specific language does not occur in the OT as such. It is a modification of the common expression for the temple, "a dwelling for his name," based on the recurring motif that Israel are a people identified with, or called by, the name of Yahweh their God. See, e.g., Num 6:27; Deut 28:10; 2 Sam 7:23; 2 Chron 7:14; Isa 43:7; Jer 14:9; Dan 9:19.

3. Cf. D. Ewert, *The Holy Spirit in the New Testament* (Harrisburg: Herald, 1983) 168, who also shows concern that by starting with the individual one may skew the data, but that if one does not take the individual into account, one will also skew Paul's overall theology. The failure to come to grips with this is one of the weaknesses of Horton's book *What the Bible Says about the Holy Spirit* (Springfield, Mo.: Gospel Publishing House, 1976). It is typical of the pietistic tradition of all strands (that is, those movements in the history of the church that have focused strongly on

individual spirituality) to read Scripture as if it were primarily written to individual believers.

4. Greek *laos*; see 2 Cor 6:16–18; Titus 2:14. Although not particularly popular with Greek writers, *laos* was the word chosen by the Septuagint (LXX) translators to render the Hebrew *'am*, the most frequently used word in the Old Testament (over two thousand times) to express the special relationship Israel had with Yahweh. Their choice of *laos* was probably because the more common word *ethnos* was used by Greek writers to refer to themselves as a people in the same way the Hebrews used *'am*. Thus for the Jews *ethnos* had come to mean "Gentile," and was so used by the LXX translators. This meant they needed a different word to distinguish themselves. [The LXX is the Greek translation of the Old Testament made in the third century BCE, and used by believers in Greek-speaking congregations. In fact, so much did the Septuagint become the Christians' Bible that by the end of the first century, Jews stopped using it altogether, and at least three other Greek translations were made for Jews in the second century.]

5. Greek *eklektos* and cognates; see 1 Thess 1:4; 2 Thess 2:13; Col 3:12; Eph 1:4, 11. As in the Old Testament the term refers not to individual election but to a people who have been chosen by God for his purposes. As one has been incorporated into, and thus belongs to, the chosen people of God, one is in that sense also elect.

6. Although "children" is the more appropriate translation into modern English, I keep "sons" in quotes because the whole passage is a play on this language. Through *the* Son we have received adoption as "sons," the evidence of which is our use of the Son's own address to the Father.

7. On the significance of this cry for the individual believer, see ch. 8 below, pp. 90–91.

8. See 1 Cor 3:16–17; 2 Cor 6:16; Eph 2:19–22; 1 Tim 3:15–16.

9. See 1 Cor 10:16–17; 11:29; 12:12–27; Rom 12:4–5; Col 1:18; 3:15; Eph 1:23; 2:16; 4:3–16; 5:23. For the most recent discussion of the imagery in Paul, see G. L. O. R. Yorke, *The Church as the Body of Christ in the Pauline Corpus: A Re-examination* (Lanham, Md.: University Press of America, 1991), whose primary conclusion is undoubtedly correct: that Paul knows nothing of a "mystical body of Christ" to which believers are joined; rather, Paul's use of the imagery is figurative in every case and has the human body as its point of reference.

CONVERSION: GETTING IN (PART 1)—THE SPIRIT AND THE HEARING OF THE GOSPEL

*Although the goal of salvation in Christ is a
people for God's name, people enter this community
one at a time. Almost every aspect of getting
in is the work of the Spirit, beginning with
the proclamation and revelation of the gospel.*

In the late eighth century, Charlemagne, king of the Franks, became a Christian; through his "persuasion" the whole Frankish nation became "Christians" and were baptized en masse. The question: Were all of these people saved? Again I would answer: Only God knows; but probably not all, for such "salvation" also lies totally outside the New Testament frame of reference. After all, it is not baptism that identifies one as a believer in Christ, but the presence of the Holy Spirit in one's life.

If the goal of salvation in Christ is a people for God's name, in continuity with the former covenant, discontinuity lies with how the people are now constituted, in two significant ways: (1) through the death and resurrection of Christ and the appropriating work of the Spirit; and (2) by entering individually, including people from every "tribe and nation."

Christ's saving work begins in the heart of the individual believer, as the appropriating work of the Spirit makes clear. After all, this emphasis on the individual is not the product of the Renaissance and Reformation—although at times these have resulted in an unfortunate and unbiblical focus on the individual. The significance of the individual before God is already in place in the Old Testament, as anyone who has lived long with the Psalter well knows. In Paul's case, the new place for the individual, as the way one "gets in," arises primarily from his altered eschatological perspective that includes Jew and Gentile alike on the same grounds. We now turn our attention to this individualized aspect of salvation in Christ,

> *"Getting saved" has to do with faith in Christ that also includes "faithfulness" to Christ.*

what it means for the believer to enter the people of God; and here the work of the Spirit looms large in Paul.

We should also note that for Paul salvation in Christ includes *both* getting in, the concern of this chapter and the next, *and* staying in, the concern of chapters 9 and 10. That is, getting saved has to do with faith in Christ that also includes faithfulness[1] to Christ. One's whole life involves trusting in Christ, who by the Spirit continually transforms us into the likeness of God. One gets in in order to stay in, and salvation for Paul includes the whole process, not simply the beginning point.

Thus these four chapters (7–10) belong together as one chapter in God's story, which is the reason for the deliberate use of the word "conversion" in the title of each. Too long the church has understood "conversion" as having only to do with the beginning point. Biblically understood, conversion has to do with making *disciples* of former pagans like ourselves (even if we were born into Christian homes, we need to be "converted" in this sense). Our Lord did not say, "Go and make converts," but "Go and make disciples." In the long run, only disciples are converts.

But conversion has a beginning point, and that is our present concern. In this chapter we look at the role of the Spirit that is more external to the believer (although nothing is so totally); in the next chapter we look at the believer's own experience of this beginning point.

THE SPIRIT AND GETTING IN

Several components make up one's experience of salvation: hearing the gospel, faith, various images of conversion, the gift of the Spirit, and baptism in water. The Spirit plays the central role in most of the process—except for baptism, which is understandable, since Paul (apparently) understood baptism as the human response to the prior divine activity.

Hearing the Gospel

For Paul Christian life begins with hearing the gospel, which both precedes faith (Rom 10:14) and is accompanied by faith (1 Thess 2:13; 2 Thess 2:13–14; Eph 1:13). "How," he asks, "can they believe in the one of whom they have not heard? And how can they hear without someone preaching to them? And how can they preach unless they are sent?" (Rom 10:14–15 NIV). This view of hearing the gospel accounts in part for Paul's own missionary urgencies. Our interest is in the role of the Spirit in this hearing of God's good news.

Two things are involved here: the gospel as God's very word (1 Thess 2:13) and therefore the truth that must be believed/trusted[2] (2 Thess 2:13; 1 Tim 2:4), revealed as such by the Spirit; and the dual act of preaching and responding, which are also the work of the Spirit.

The Spirit and Preaching

In 2 Corinthians 3:8, Paul contrasts his own ministry with that of Moses, and indirectly with that of the "peddlers of another Jesus." In doing so, he refers to his own ministry as "the ministry of the Spirit," meaning the ministry of the new covenant, which is empowered by the Spirit and results in others' receiving the Spirit.

Such ministry, he insists, despite the earthenware vessel through which it comes, is accompanied by far greater glory than that which accompanied the ministry of Moses in the former covenant. The far greater glory, it turns out in this context, is the work of the Spirit, who brings us into the presence of the living God. He does so by removing the veil that keeps people from beholding God's glory in the face of Christ Jesus and consequently from being transformed into his likeness.

Paul refers frequently to his own effective ministry as a direct result of the work of the Spirit. This work included not only conviction concerning the truth of the gospel, but also signs and wonders, all of which resulted in changed lives. Indeed, the first reference to the Spirit in Paul's writings (1 Thess 1:5-6) strikes this note. Paul begins his encouragement of this new—and suf-fering—Christian community by reminding them of two Spirit-experienced realities: his ministry among them, and the nature of their conversion.

They became followers of Christ (v. 5) not on the basis of Paul's proclamation of the gospel alone, but because that proclamation was accompanied by the power of the Spirit, including a deep conviction (probably both in Paul as he preached and in them as they heard). Whether the power of the Spirit in this instance also included accompanying signs and wonders is moot (I think it did; Rom 15:18-19 indicates that such was regularly the case). The Thessalonians' reception of the gospel was accompanied by much affliction and by the joy of the Holy Spirit (v. 6), that unquench-able joy the Spirit brings to those who have come to know the living and true God (v. 9).

So also with 1 Corinthians 2:1-5. In defending his ministry in Corinth against his opponents (cf. 4:1-21; 9:1-2), Paul in this paragraph takes up the matter of his preaching when he first came to the city. Both the content (1:18-25) and the form (2:1-5) of his preaching lacked persuasive wisdom and rhetoric; nonetheless, his preaching was far more effective than wisdom or rhetoric, Paul argues. It was accompanied by a demonstration of the *Spirit's* power, proved by the conversion of the Corinthians themselves (cf. 2 Cor 3:3). And it was so, Paul adds, in order that their faith might rest in "the power of God," not in merely human wisdom.

These passages, and the next, make clear that Paul understood Christian conversion to begin with Spirit-empowered proclamation, which by the same Spirit found its lodging in the heart of the hearer so as to bring conviction—of sin (as in 1 Cor 14:24–25), as well as of the truth of the gospel.

But the Spirit's role in Paul's preaching was not limited to an "anointing" of Paul's own words, thus carrying conviction as to the truth of the gospel. In Romans 15:18–19 he insists that his preaching all the way from Jerusalem to Illyricum was an effective combination of "word *and* deed," both of which were by "the power of the Spirit." By "word" he refers to his preaching; he explains "deed" as referring to "signs and wonders through the power of the Spirit."

For Paul this double display of power (empowered words and powerful deeds) forms the foundation for his understanding of the role of the promised Spirit. That is, he never argues *for* such empowering, nor does he allow anyone to authenticate either his ministry or their faith on that basis (2 Cor 5:13). But neither would he understand the presence of the promised Spirit without such a double expression of power. We are dealing with the Spirit of God, after all, the present eschatological fulfillment of God's empowering presence. It would never occur to him that the miraculous would *not* accompany the proclamation of the gospel, or that in another time some would think of these two empowerings as "either-or." For Paul, it is simply a matter of, "of course." Thus, speaking of his ministry as a whole, he can confidently say to the Colossians, "to which end also I labor, contending for the gospel in keeping with God's being at work in me with power" (1:29), by which he means "by the power of the Spirit."

What is true of Paul's own ministry he also understands to be true of the effective preaching of the gospel in general. "And take the sword of the Spirit," he urges in Ephesians 6:17, meaning, to "speak forth the word of God" (the truth about Christ) in a world where the powers are still at work. Thus he urges them to be involved in a Spirit-empowered proclamation of Christ.

Similarly, this understanding of the relationship of the Spirit to ministry lies behind three passages addressed to Timothy (1 Tim 1:18; 4:14; 2 Tim 1:6–7; cf. v. 14), in which Paul recalls Timothy's experience of "call" to ministry. Because of context, each text emphasizes a different aspect of that experience.

1. Timothy's gift *(charisma)* refers first to the Spirit (2 Tim 1:6–7), but is also broadened to refer to the gift of ministry that came by the Spirit (1 Tim 4:14). The experience therefore is something that happened to (within) Timothy. He experienced a Spirit-directed, Spirit-given "call," singling him out for the ministry of the gospel.

2. The experience, however, took place in a community setting of some kind, since it also came by way of prophetic utterances spoken about and to him (1 Tim 1:18; 4:14). Indeed, in 1:18 Paul appeals to the content of these "calling" words from the Lord, which came through others in the community, as his means of bolstering Timothy's courage to do battle in a very trying situation in Ephesus.

3. The community of elders responded to this work of the Spirit by the laying on of hands (4:14; 2 Tim 1:6; cf. the similar sequence in Acts 13:1–3). The gift itself did not come through their laying on of hands; rather, their act was one of recognition and affirmation of the prior work of the Spirit that had come through prophetic utterances. The Spirit as an *experienced* reality is the obvious key to these appeals.

REVELATION BY THE SPIRIT

Part of Paul's conviction that his message was, and would be, accompanied by the Spirit's power was his corresponding conviction that the essential content of the gospel came to him by revelation,[3] again as the work of the Spirit. Both 1 Corinthians 2:10–16 and Ephesians 3:5–7 affirm that his own insight into the gospel came by the Spirit's revelation.

This revelation involved a twofold unveiling of God's mystery. First, in 1 Corinthians 2:6–16 the Spirit is understood to have revealed what was formerly hidden—and is still hidden to those without the Spirit. Only by the Spirit (v. 10) could he and his converts understand what the human mind could not conceive (v. 9), namely, that God in his own wisdom had chosen to redeem our fallen race through the crucifixion of Christ. Thus Paul's preaching of the cross came with "words taught by the Spirit" (v. 13), which included "explaining Spiritual things by Spiritual means" (= the things taught by the Spirit with language appropriate to the Spirit). To have the Spirit in this way means not to be subject to merely human judgments; rather, it means to have the mind of Christ (vv. 15–16; cf. 7:25, 40).

The gospel at its profoundest point stands in utter contradiction to human wisdom: God has redeemed our fallen race by means of the ultimate contradiction in terms, a crucified Messiah.

Pivotal to Paul's argument is that this revelation should be the common experience of all who have received the Spirit. Paul's problem with the Corinthians was that they considered themselves to be people of the Spirit, yet were abandoning the cross for human wisdom and rhetoric. Hence the vital role of the Spirit, who reveals to those who love God what was formerly hidden (1 Cor 2:9–10), namely, what God in Christ has freely given us (v. 12).

It is not some obscure secret wisdom that has been revealed by the Spirit, but the content of the gospel, God's "mystery." The need for revelation by the Spirit at this point is considerable, since it requires an understanding that merely human wisdom could never penetrate. The gospel at its profoundest point stands in utter contradiction to human wisdom: God has redeemed our fallen race by means of the ultimate contradiction in terms, a crucified Messiah. Without the Spirit, who alone knows the mind of God, human beings do not stand a chance to penetrate this "hidden mystery," which "eye has not seen nor has it entered into the heart of human beings." The Corinthians should have recognized this, precisely because they, too, had received the Spirit that they might be taught by means of the Spirit the things of the Spirit. But they were caught up in a false "Spirituality" that was leading them in "all glory now" directions, thus sidestepping discipleship marked by the cross (see ch. 12 below).

Second, in Ephesians 3:2–13 this mystery, God's hidden wisdom now revealed by the Spirit, includes the fact that "Gentiles are heirs together with Israel, members together of one body, and sharers together in the promise in Christ Jesus" (v. 6). Since these words reflect the primary focus of the argument of Galatians and Romans as well, it is not surprising that Paul here speaks of these matters in terms of "revelation" that came "by the Spirit." Therefore for Paul both the revelation of the inclusion of Jews and Gentiles together in Christ and their actual inclusion (1:13–14; 2:18, 22) are the work of the Spirit. Such inclusion in the present time obviously needs the revelation that only the eschatological Spirit can bestow, since most Jews were looking for this fulfillment at the End, and in terms of "nations" rather than "individuals."

What required revelation was not that Gentiles were to be included in the promised end-time blessings of God—that was commonly accepted by all—but that they would be included Torah-free (that is, free from the observances of the Jewish law) and on equal grounds with Jews, so that God in Christ had formed one new humanity of the two peoples (Eph 2:14–15). Such an understanding could have come only by the Spirit's revelation, both through Jews' and Gentiles' common experience of the Spirit (1 Cor 12:13) and through a conscious understanding of what Christ and the Spirit had done (Eph 3:5).

A further aspect of revelation connected with the hearing of the gospel occurs in 1 Corinthians 14:24–25. Here the revelation comes by means of prophetic utterances within the believing community when unbelievers are present. What is revealed in this case are the secrets of the unbelievers' hearts, leading them (apparently) to repentance and conversion.

We should pause here to note that in the present overview of Paul's theology, focusing as we are on the role of the Spirit in that theology, there is no mention of the human predicament that made salvation a necessity. This is because Paul sees not the Holy Spirit, but the evil spirit, Satan, as at work in those whose minds he "has blinded so that they cannot behold the light of the gospel in face of God's glory, Christ himself" (2 Cor 4:4). Believers can see the glory because the Spirit has removed the veil, in this case the "blindfold." The 1 Corinthians passage indicates in part at least how the Spirit removes the veil—by means of a prophetic utterance that penetrates into the unbeliever's heart and lays it bare before all.

The Spirit appears both as the one who initiates our faith and as the one who is received by that same faith.

The "revelation" in this case has probably to do with the unbeliever's sinfulness, which in turn leads him or her to hear the greater revelation that has taken place in Christ. Such revelation by the prophetic Spirit serves for believers as the sure sign of God's favor and presence among them (1 Cor 14:22). All this is the work of the Spirit.

It is clear from all this that the conversion of the individual believer begins with a sovereign act of God, carried out by the Holy Spirit. As Paul put it, "How can they call on the one they have not believed in? And how can they believe in the one of whom they have not heard? And how can hear without someone preaching to them? And how can they preach unless they are sent?" (Rom 10:14–15 NIV). God's action is clearly the prior one.

In the divine mystery of things our "believing" (or "trusting") is the hinge point between our "calling on God" and our "hearing the gospel." Our trusting, which is the point at which what is external to us becomes internal, is in some mysterious way the working of the Holy Spirit as both cause and effect. That is, the Spirit appears both as the one who initiates our faith and as the one who is received by that same faith; and that is the starting point of the next chapter.

NOTES

1. The one word, *pistis,* expresses for Paul both of these ideas: trust, and trusting faithfulness. Thus *pistis* is listed among the fruit of the Spirit

(Gal 5:22), as well as serving to denote our proper response to God's saving grace.

2. The Greek word variously translated "faith," "belief," or "trust" is a difficult one to render into English by a single word. Our words tends to be too limiting; "belief," for example, puts the emphasis on what goes on in our heads. The Greek word includes that, but means to put one's trust in that which one "believes."

3. On this question, both as to its Jewish background and its Pauline usage, see especially M. Bockmuehl, *Revelation and Mystery in Ancient Judaism and Pauline Christianity* (WUNT 2/36; Tübingen: J. C. B. Mohr [Paul Siebeck], 1990). My interest at this point is in "revelation" as it refers to Paul's—and his churches'—hearing and understanding the gospel. But in keeping with his view of salvation as all-inclusive, having to do with both getting in and staying in, revelation becomes part of Christian life, as God's people, by the Spirit, come to discern God's will for their ethical life. See the further discussion in chs. 9 and 10 below.

CONVERSION: GETTING IN (PART 2)—THE SPIRIT AT THE ENTRY POINT

"Getting in," which begins with the hearing of the gospel, is appropriated by faith and includes an experience of "receiving" the Holy Spirit.

"How do you feel?" Trevor was asked, following his response to hearing the gospel and having asked Christ to come into his life. "Wonderful," he responded; "I feel like a new person." "That's great," came the reply. But also with the reply came the first cautionary words he would learn as a new believer in Christ. "But don't trust your feelings; your salvation is not based on how you feel, but on the truth of what Christ has done for you. You will have to learn to trust his word, because the feelings may not always be there."

This is a common conversation for us, and full of truth and wisdom. What is hard to imagine is Paul ever having such a conversation with *his* new converts. In Galatians 3:1–5, when he encourages them to stay with "faith in Christ" and not get entangled with "works of law," he first appeals not to the truth of the gospel, but to their experience of the Spirit by which they started on the path of Christian discipleship. This is not an appeal to feelings but to something common to them all—the *experienced* reality of their conversion to Christ through the coming of the Spirit.

Although he would not have used such language, for Paul Christian conversion has both an objective and a subjective dimension to it. On the one hand, Christ's death and resurrection have secured eternal salvation for those who believe. This objective, historical reality is conveyed with various figures of speech, each of which emphasizes a significant aspect of the believer's new relationship with God (redemption, reconciliation, washing, propitiation, justification, adoption, birth). At the entry point of conversion, this objective historical reality becomes an objective personal reality for the believer as well, in terms of her or his position in God through Christ. As Charles Wesley sang (marvelously):

Arise, my soul arise,
  Shake off thy guilty fears;
The bleeding sacrifice
  In my behalf appears;
Before the throne my Surety stands,
  My name is written on His hands.

But for Paul the beginning point of conversion also involves a clearly subjective, personally experienced dimension that results in some radical changes in the believer; and the Spirit is the absolutely indispensable element for this dimension. As H. B. Swete put it, "Without the mission of the Spirit the mission of the Son would have been fruitless; without the mission of the Son the Spirit could not have been sent."[1] That Paul held the Spirit to play such a key role in the subjective side of conversion can be shown in several ways, beginning with our trust in Christ.

THE SPIRIT AND FAITH

The relationship of the Spirit to faith in Paul's letters is not an easy one to sort out.[2] On the one hand, in Galatians 3:2–5 Paul states firmly that the gift of the Spirit comes through "faith in Christ Jesus." According to any systematic presentation, this suggests that faith itself precedes the reception of the Spirit. On the other hand, in 1 Corinthians 12:8 and 13:2 faith is considered one of the evidences of the Spirit at work. If these passages can be dismissed as referring (correctly so) to that unusual gift of faith that accompanies the miraculous, the same can scarcely be said of the faith that is the fruit of the Spirit (Gal 5:22). Here faith refers to "saving faith" in its continuing expression of "faithfulness." So also in 2 Corinthians 4:13, Paul refers to "having the same Spirit who effects faith as the psalmist had," who leads us "to believe."

This prompts me to suggest that faith itself, as a work of the Spirit, leads us to receive and experience the Spirit who also comes through that same faith. Although it does not fit our logical schemes well, the Spirit is thus both the cause and the effect of faith. This same close relationship of the Spirit to faith is also presupposed in Galatians 5:5, where Paul urges that *we,* in contrast to *them* (the Jewish Christian agitators), "by the Spirit, on the basis of faith, await the final righteousness for which we hope." The object of faith, as always, is Christ; the Spirit is the means whereby such faith is sustained.

What all of this means, then, drawing on our conclusion from chapter 7, is that for Paul both the understanding of the gospel and the event of preaching, including the hearing that leads to faith, are the work of the Spirit. In this sense one may legitimately argue that faith itself is also a prior work of the Spirit in the life of the one who becomes a believer, since "we have the same Spirit who inspires faith" so that "we believe" (2 Cor 4:13). It is equally clear from the evidence that "faith" is not all there is to it.

THE CRUCIAL ROLE OF THE SPIRIT IN CONVERSION[3]

That something "happens" to the one who puts his or her trust in Christ is not simply the presupposition of revivalist preaching. It is the clear understanding of Paul, who wrote all of his letters before there was a second generation, those who grew up as the children of believing parents. The first generation, those to whom his letters were addressed, were for the most part converts to Christ from paganism. His own encounter with Christ, even though it meant fulfillment of his hopes rather than conversion from another religion, had a clearly experiential quality to it. Such an experiential dimension of entry into Christian life was therefore both his presupposition and what happened to others when he preached.

The Spirit at the Beginning Point

"Did you receive the Spirit by Torah observance, or by believing what you heard? Are you so foolish? Having begun by the Spirit, are you now trying to come to completion through the flesh?" This is the question with which Paul confronts the Galatians (3:2–3), to bring them up short in their readiness to be persuaded by Jewish Christian agitators to be circumcised. Notice he does not put it our way, "Were you saved, or justified, and so on?" His question works precisely because of the *experiential* nature of their having received the Spirit, as the present-tense question in v. 5 makes certain: "He who supplies you with the Spirit and performs miracles among you, is this by faith or by doing the law?" For Paul the Spirit is the crucial element to *all* of Christian life; therefore his argument stands or falls on their recalling their own experience of conversion at the *beginning* in terms of the Spirit.

For Paul, therefore, whatever else happens at Christian conversion, it is the experience of the Spirit that is crucial; and therefore it is the Spirit alone who identifies God's people in the present eschatological age.

The Spirit plays the same vital role in several other passages where Paul describes his readers' turning to Christ in terms of what has happened to the believer (1 Cor 12:13; Eph 1:13–14; Titus 3:5–7). So also with all sorts of texts where, quite in passing, he reminds them of their beginnings in Christ. For example, God gave them his Spirit

(Rom 5:5), anointed them with the Spirit (2 Cor 1:21), poured out his Spirit generously on them (Titus 3:6), and sealed them with the Spirit (Eph 1:13; 4:30). Believers have received the Spirit (1 Cor 2:12; 2 Cor 11:4), been saved through the sanctifying work of the Spirit (2 Thess 2:13; Rom 15:16), been circumcised in their hearts by the Spirit (Rom 2:29), and been joined to Christ so as to become one S/spirit with him (1 Cor 6:17). As well as "by the name of Christ," believers have been "washed, sanctified, and justified" by "the Spirit of our God" (1 Cor 6:11). In the analogy of Ishmael and Isaac in Galatians 4:29, the former is "born of the flesh," while the latter (= the Galatian believers) was born of the Spirit.

Titus 3:4–7 is significant in yet another way, since Paul here describes conversion in language that sounds much like a creed. What is remarkable is the significant role the Spirit plays in this formulation. Here the Spirit is mentioned even before the work of Christ, since the emphasis is on what has happened to the believer: God has saved them through the washing and renewing work of the Spirit, whom God lavishly poured out on them through Christ the Savior.

For Paul, therefore, whatever else happens at Christian conversion, it is the experience of the Spirit that is crucial; and therefore it is the Spirit alone who identifies God's people in the present eschatological age.

The Spirit as the Identity Marker of the Converted

In the same manner, Paul three times distinguishes believers from nonbelievers in terms of the former having the Spirit, while the latter do not (1 Cor 2:6–16; 12:3; Rom 8:9). Most significant of these is 1 Corinthians 2:6–16, where he sets out the basic contrasts between the "natural person" and the "Spiritual person." The natural person is one who does not have the Spirit and is therefore incapable of understanding what God has done through the cross; whereas the opposite is true of the believer. Likewise no one can make the basic Christian confession of Jesus as Lord, except by the Holy Spirit (1 Cor 12:3). Finally, he says it plainly,

"If anyone does not have the Spirit, that person does not belong to Christ at all" (Rom 8:9).

In a former time Paul had divided the world between "us" and "them" in terms of Jews and Gentiles. The new division is between those who belong to Christ and those who do not; and what characterizes the former is that they have the Spirit, while the others do not. Whatever else, the newly formed people of God are Spirit people. They have come to life by the life-giving Spirit (Gal 5:25; 2 Cor 3:3, 6); they walk by the Spirit, and they are led by the Spirit. For Paul, therefore, to "get saved" means first of all to "receive the Spirit."

For Paul, therefore, to "get saved" means first of all to "receive the Spirit."

THE SPIRIT AND PAUL'S IMAGES FOR SALVATION

How Paul perceives this converting work of the Spirit is best seen by looking at the various images he uses to describe salvation. The more common images are seldom used in conjunction with the Spirit. Justification is connected with the Spirit only in 1 Corinthians 6:11;[4] redemption, propitiation, and reconciliation are not at all. The reason for this is close at hand: these images emphasize the objective aspect of salvation, dealing with the believer's position or relation to God, and therefore are used exclusively to refer to Christ's saving work in our behalf, in which we put our trust. But when Paul uses metaphors that emphasize the believer's *experience* of salvation, the Spirit is then frequently mentioned.

Adoption

We have noted above in chapter 6 the use of this imagery as key to Paul's understanding the church as God's family (Gal 4:5–6). Here we note that vv. 5 and 6 together give solid evidence of the distinctions made about the objective and subjective dimensions of conversion. In v. 5 Paul refers to Christ the Son's act of redemption on the cross as securing our "adoption as 'sons' "; in v. 6 he individualizes this work in terms of the Spirit's crying *Abba*, the special language of the Son, from within the heart of the believer.

The difficulties with this text come with the way v. 6 begins. In making his new point (after vv. 4–5), Paul starts the sentence by saying that *because* they are "sons," God has sent the Spirit of his Son into their hearts. That sounds as if the one thing (objective sonship) preceded the other (the gift of the Spirit). This apparent awkwardness is the result of our reading the text as though Paul were offering a chronology of individual salvation. Verse 5, however, does not refer to the individual believer's salvation history at all. Rather, Paul here presents the work of Christ as an objective, once-for-all, historical reality, by which Christ procured "adoption" for all who would ever trust him. The experience of the individual believer is historically later than, and based upon, this prior work of Christ. Thus the cause-and-effect relationship is that between "sonship" provided for us by Christ's death on the cross and "sonship" as made real by the Spirit in the life of the believer.

That Paul has little concern for the "ordering" of things can be seen from 3:2–5 (noted above), where the Spirit alone is the key to their conversion. The same is true of the parallel in Romans 8:15–17, where the Spirit, not Christ, is mentioned as responsible for adoption. Paul's intent in both texts is simply to remind believers that their receiving of the Spirit is what *makes* them children, as is *proved* by the cry "*Abba.*"

We should not pass too quickly over the significance of this cry. *Abba* was the language of infancy, and along with *Imma* ("Mother"), the first word an Aramaic-speaking child would learn. But it was also the endearing term that children of all ages continued to use, expressing both intimacy and special relatedness. What may begin as baby talk is not thereby to be outgrown; on the contrary, it is to be grown into. That we are the beloved children of the eternal God is knowledge "shed abroad in our hearts by the Spirit" (Rom 5:5) and by that same Spirit is manifest in our lifelong cry to God as our heavenly *Abba*. Crying *Abba* to God through the Spirit of God's Son means that our relationship of utter dependence on God, lost in the fall, has been restored by the Son; we can depend on him for everything. The experience of the Spirit leads the believer not only to a position of justification before God, but also should lead to an ongoing awareness of the privileges of childhood—personal relationship and companionship with God himself. Being "in the presence of God" through Christ and by the Spirit (2 Cor 2:17; Eph 2:18) was for Paul a cause not for fear but for confidence.

Washing, Rebirth, Giving Life

These three images need to be examined together, partly because in some cases they occur in the same texts and partly because some issues raised by them belong in discussion together.

1. The image of "washing" as a work of the Spirit first occurs in 1 Corinthians 6:11. Many see here a reference to baptism, especially because it is followed by the phrase "in the name of the Lord Jesus Christ," which is considered a baptismal formula. But this interpretation runs aground both on Paul's usage elsewhere and on the structure of the sentence, where both prepositions modify all three verbs.[5] That is, "in the name of our Lord Jesus" and "by the Spirit of our God" together modify the three verbs "washed, sanctified, justified." Although this expression may indirectly allude to baptism, in context the emphasis falls on the image of "washing away of sin," especially those sins just mentioned in vv. 9–10. Our point is that the Spirit is specifically singled out as the means of such cleansing.

This image occurs again, along with the images of "rebirth" and "renewal," in Titus 3:5. As the central feature of salvation Paul says (literally), "God saved us . . . through washing of rebirth and renewal of the Holy Spirit." Although there are some inherent difficulties with this phrase, the evidence points most strongly to an interpretation that sees this not as referring to two experiences (the washing of rebirth and the renewal of the Spirit = baptism and confirmation, or conversion and Spirit baptism), but to one (a washing that involves rebirth and renewal, all of which are put into effect by the Spirit).[6]

But opinion is also divided among those who take this position. Does "washing" refer to water baptism or more simply to the "washing away of sin," and what relationship does the Spirit have to this washing? Again, we need not doubt that it probably alludes to baptism; but that Paul uses a figure of speech and not the word "baptism" implies that his own emphasis is on the figure, not on the event of baptism. The final phrase, "of the Spirit," is the key to the whole. Salvation is not received through baptism—that is foreign to Paul—but through the work of the Spirit, which in this case is represented as a "new birth" (cf. John 3:3) or a "renewal" in the new believer's life.

2. The two expressions "new birth" and "renewal" are as close as we get to the concept of "regeneration" by the Spirit in Paul's writings. But if this concept is infrequent, the idea behind it is not foreign to Paul. We begin the Christian walk, having been given life by the Spirit (see below). Such new life is likewise pictured as a renewal (cf. Rom 12:2; Col 3:10).

Absolutely basic to Paul's understanding of becoming a believer in Christ, therefore, is not simply that we are given a new objective standing with God—redeemed, forgiven, cleansed, "justified"—but that we are also "washed . . . by the Spirit," which includes rebirth and renewal. By the Spirit God cleanses people from past sins; by the Spirit God also transforms them into his people, "reborn" and "renewed" to reflect God's likeness in their lives.

Paul understands a radical change to have taken place at the beginning point of conversion; it means a complete reorientation of our entire lives. This reorientation is directly tied to the work of the Spirit. Theologically we may refer to this as a rebirth, even though this image is not central in Paul's view of things. For him, because his primary focus is always on the work of Christ, what happens to the believer is "death" and "resurrection" (2 Cor 5:14; Gal 5:24; Rom 6:1-6; Col 2:20–3:4). And this is where conversion as the experience of the "life-giving Spirit" comes in.

3. Whatever else may be said about God in the Old Testament, the main reality about him, which is revealed even in his name, is that Yahweh is the living and life-giving God. That God lives and gives life to all that lives is foundational to biblical faith. What is

crucial to Paul's understanding of Christian conversion is that the Spirit whom believers receive is none other than the "Spirit of life" (Rom 8:2, 6), who "gives life" to those who turn to Christ (2 Cor 3:6). For Paul the old (flesh, sin, Torah observance) has been crucified (Gal 5:24); we have been raised with Christ to live in "the newness of the Spirit" (Rom 7:6). "If anyone is in Christ, *a new creation*," he exclaims (2 Cor 5:17); "the old (life 'according to the flesh') is gone; the new (life 'according to the Spirit') has come."

This is why from Paul's perspective Christian conversion also includes walking in "newness of life." Thus, following his statement that the flesh was crucified with Christ, he implores that "if we live (following our crucifixion with Christ) by the Spirit, then let us also behave in keeping with the self-same Spirit" (Gal 5:25). For Paul there is no such thing as a believer who is not thereby brought to life—life now and forever—by the coming of the life-giving Spirit. Such life manifests itself in the radically new life of God given by the Spirit.

Paul's understanding of Christian conversion as essentially the work of the Spirit, therefore, has no place in it for the whitewashed sinner, the person who is still sinful, but justified before God anyway. The only coming to Christ known to Paul is one in which the life of the believer has been invaded by the life-giving Spirit, who both applies the redemptive work of the cross and also transforms us from within, by the "renewing of the mind" (Rom 12:2). All of Paul's metaphors of "before" and "after" speak in the same way of the radical transformation of life that the Spirit brings (death/life; old *anthrōpos* [person]/new person; darkness/light; etc.), which is brought into focus by the next image as well.

Sanctification

Paul's primary use of the term "sanctification" is also as a figure of speech for conversion, not a reference to a work of grace *following* conversion. This can be seen most clearly in 2 Thessalonians 2:13, where Paul refers to the Thessalonians' experience of salvation as being brought about "by sanctification of the Spirit and belief in the truth."

The image is drawn from Jewish religious practices, where the sacred rites and utensils have become so by their having been sanctified unto God, that is, set apart solely for God's holy purposes. This same use of the image, referring now especially to Gentile conversions under Paul's ministry, occurs in Romans 15:16. The Jewish Christians in Rome may not call "common or unclean" (because of failure to be circumcised) those whom God has sanctified by the Spirit. The Gentiles' reception of the Spirit was God's ultimate act of creating for himself a sanctified offering composed of both Gentile and Jew.

On the other hand, the use of the same imagery to refer to the Corinthians' conversion (1 Cor 6:11) is intended to emphasize that conversion includes the sanctifying work of the Spirit which prohibits the kind of behavior in which they formerly engaged. "Such *were* some of you," he asserts, "but you have been . . . sanctified . . . by the Spirit of our God."

———

Adding to these the images of "anointing," "seal," "down payment," and "firstfruits" (see ch. 5 above), one can draw firm conclusions:

1. The wide variety of images and figures of speech in itself indicates that no single one will do. The work of Christ, applied by the Spirit in Christian conversion, simply has too many facets to be captured by a single image. In almost every case the choice of images is related to the perspective on the human condition that is addressed in the context. Thus, propitiation responds to our being under God's wrath; redemption to our being enslaved to sin; justification to our guilt before God's law; reconciliation to our being God's enemies; sanctification to our being unholy; washing to our being unclean; and so on.

2. The images tend to be used in keeping with the emphasis of the moment, thus the point in context is what is at issue, not the precise timing or relationships in conversion.

3. There is no such thing as Christian conversion that does not have the coming of the Spirit into the believer's life as the critical ingredient. However variously expressed, the presence of the Spirit is the one constant.

But all has not been said. Does the evidence of this chapter mean that those who, when coming to faith in Christ, did not have an *experiential* realization of the Spirit's presence therefore fall short of biblical faith? Not for a minute. All of us who trust Christ have received the Spirit, even if the coming of the gift was more quiescent. The point of this chapter for today's believer is that the Spirit, and the Spirit alone, not only gets us on our way in Christ but also is what Christian life is finally all about.

There is no such thing as Christian conversion that does not have the coming of the Spirit into the believer's life as the critical ingredient.

That the coming of the Spirit in the Pauline churches was a more experiential reality than is true for many of us probably has a lot to do with their expectations. For some of us it may also be related to being second-generation Christians. As has often been said, "God has no grandchildren." So when do we *experience* the Spirit? Such an experiential way of entry is still common in many parts of the world. What we may say with confidence is that even though we may not have begun that way, we may still enter into a much more experienced life in the Spirit than is perhaps now the case. In this regard the Spirit has not changed.

More also needs to be said about the Spirit's role in salvation in Christ, because Paul would not understand conversion that did not include growing up into Christ. For him the Spirit was the essential ingredient to the whole of life in Christ. So, what does the converted person looks like? What does it mean to become a Spirit person—one who not only begins with the Spirit but walks in the Spirit? That is the subject of the next two chapters.

NOTES

1. See H. B. Swete, *The Holy Spirit in the New Testament* (1910; repr. ed. Grand Rapids: Baker, 1964) 206.

2. See the discussion in *GEP* on 1 Cor 12:8; 13:2; 2 Cor 4:13; Gal 3:1–5.

3. The texts here are many and varied; see, e.g., the discussions in *GEP* on 1 Thess 1:4-6; 2 Thess 2:13; 1 Cor 2:6-3:1; 6:11, 19-20; 2 Cor 1:21-22; 3:1-18; 11:4; 13:13[14]; Gal 3:1-5; 4:6; 5:5-6; 5:13-6:10; Rom 5:5; 7:4-6; 8:1-30; 14:16-18; 15:13, 16; Eph 1:3-14; 4:1-6, 30; Phil 3:3; Titus 3:4-7.

4. Most likely in terms of the believer's appropriation. Cf. Rom 14:17, although here the connection is only indirectly made (see *GEP*, 620-21 and n. 449).

5. See the analysis of this verse in *GEP*, 127-32.

6. See *GEP*, 777-84.

CONVERSION: STAYING IN (PART 1)—THE SPIRIT AND PAULINE ETHICS

*The Spirit, in constituting a new people for God's name,
fulfills the purpose of the law and stands over against
the "flesh" by enabling righteous living.*

I grew up in a church where the buzz phrases "eternal security" and "once saved, always saved" were bad news. People who believed so, I was told, even if they did not intend it, encouraged "easy-believism" and "cheap grace"; that is, people believed in Christ for salvation but failed to exhibit it in their lives. They were eternally secure, so why get uptight about how they lived? Only later did I learn that this language was a popular distortion of Calvin's perseverance of the saints. Calvin believed (rightly so) that God enables his holy ones, his saints, to persevere to the end, and in that sense they were secure—eternally. Unfortunately, what was sometimes advocated as Calvinism often did offer false security to *un*believers, people who wanted a passport to heaven without becoming citizens.[1]

Nothing could be further from Paul's perspective. Salvation has to do with both getting in and staying in. To get saved means to be joined to the people of God by the Spirit; and to be saved means to live the life of the saved person. We are brought to life by the Spirit so as to live the life of heaven on earth, also by the Spirit—walking in the Spirit, being led by the Spirit, sowing to the

We are brought to life by the Spirit so as to live the life of heaven on earth, also by the Spirit—walking in the Spirit, being led by the Spirit, sowing to the Spirit.

Spirit. The Spirit who implants the faith by which we believe (2 Cor 4:13) is the same Spirit whose fruit in our lives includes faith (Gal 5:22), meaning now "faithful walking in God's ways." Merely optional righteousness is unthinkable.

What does it mean, then, to live in the Christian community and in the world as the people of God? That is what ethics is all about, which is what this chapter is all about. To be sure, life in the Spirit means far more than just ethical behavior. The whole of life under the new covenant is now lived in and by the Spirit, including worship, one's relationship to God, and everyday life itself. But since ethical life is often central in his letters, and since the Spirit is mentioned often in these contexts, Paul's understanding of Christian ethics as life in the Spirit is the focus of this chapter.[2]

THE SPIRIT AND ETHICAL LIFE

For many people Christian behavior is a rather straightforward affair. They read Paul's various imperatives (commands) as a new form of law and try their best to abide by them, giving each command much the same value. Love for neighbor and the wearing of head coverings, forgiveness and women keeping silent in church, sexual purity and what you eat or drink, all carry the same weight. Even though we are saved by grace, God expects us to live according to his commands in every aspect of our lives. But such a view is both too easy and too hard, and a poor reading of Paul.

First of all, it is too easy because it is purely individualistic. It is far easier to be a Christian in isolation than it is to live out one's faith in the context of all those other imperfect people who make up God's church. It is too easy precisely because it turns Christian ethics into easily performed codes of conduct having to do not with caring for one another but with penny-ante stuff like food and drink. At the same time it is too hard, because it thinks of ethics in terms of law and finds forgiving wrongdoing and loving the unlovely impossible; such ethics totally misses the glorious freedom of the children of God to live the life of the future together, empowered by the Spirit.

Two issues, therefore, confront us in this chapter. First, that Christian ethics is not primarily an individualistic, one-on-one-with-God brand of personal holiness; rather it has to do with living the life of the Spirit in Christian community and in the world. As with getting in, Paul's accent here falls heavily on the community. His concern is with the local church as the people of God in their city. Hence most of his instructions to them are in the second person plural, with the whole church in mind. But these instructions are expressed in such a way that they are experienced and obeyed at the individual level. For example, the command to remain filled with the Spirit in Ephesians 5:18 is addressed to a community setting in which believers teach one another with various kinds of songs. By the very nature of things, it applies first to individual believers, who must respond to the exhortation if the community is to be filled with the Spirit.

The whole of life under the new covenant is now lived in and by the Spirit, including worship, one's relationship to God, and everyday life itself.

The second issue is that ethics has to do with life *in the Spirit*, not life disguised as such though really a continuation of life under law. In saving us through Christ and the Spirit, God has created an eschatological people, who live the life of the future in the present, a life reflecting the character of the God who became present first in Christ and then by his Spirit. As the renewed presence of God, the Spirit, having given life to his people, now leads them in paths of righteousness for his name's sake.

Part of this second issue has to do with the role of the law in Pauline ethics. For whenever Paul wrestles theologically with "works of law" and "justification by grace," he invariably brings in the Spirit as the key to the question, What happens to righteousness in terms of behavior, if righteousness is by grace apart from the law? Since some of what Paul says on this matter seems ambiguous to many people, we will begin our look at "Spirit ethics" by first trying to resolve this issue.

The Spirit and the New Covenant

Even though it was God's presence that distinguished Israel as God's own people, their identity as that people was bound up with their obedience to the Torah, the law. Itinerant Jewish Christians were forever dogging Paul's heels, entering his churches and arguing that for believers in Christ to be identified with God's people they must also observe Torah. On the contrary, Paul argues, the Spirit, and the Spirit alone, identifies the people of God under the new covenant.

The failure of the former covenant, the covenant of law, was that even though the Torah was "Spiritual" in the sense that it came by way of Spirit-inspiration (Rom 7:14), and even though it came with glory (2 Cor 3:7), it was not accompanied by the empowering Spirit. Indeed, it was written on stone tablets, which for Paul represented its deadness, its basic inability to set people free. It had become a covenant of letter (a merely written code of laws requiring obedience) leading to death (Rom 2:29; 7:6; 2 Cor 3:5–6); and a veil like that which covered Moses' face to hide the fading glory now covers the hearts of all who hear it read (2 Cor 3:14).

In contrast, the new covenant, by means of the life-giving Spirit, is written on "tablets of human hearts" (2 Cor 3:3); its rite of "circumcision" is by the Spirit and "of the heart" (Rom 2:29). The gospel and its ministry are accompanied by a much greater and more enduring glory, the ministry of the Spirit himself (2 Cor 3:8). The new covenant is life-giving, because its content, Christ, is administered by the Spirit. It is through the Spirit that we behold—and are being transformed into—the glory of the Lord (2 Cor 3:4–18). The promised new covenant has replaced the old, and the gift of the Spirit proves it.

Essential to this view of things is Paul's understanding of the gift of the Spirit as fulfillment of the new covenant promise of Jeremiah 31:31–34, which had come to be read in light of Ezekiel 36:26–37:14. The reason for a new covenant was the failure of the old to produce a truly meaningful righteousness, a righteousness coming from an obedient heart, rather than dutiful observances—as though God's people could be identified by circumcision, the observance of days, and food laws. The Old Testament itself is abundantly clear that God's intent with Torah was for his character to be revealed in the way his people worshipped and lived,[3] hence the crucial role to be played by the Spirit.

The Old Testament itself is abundantly clear that God's intent with Torah was for his character to be revealed in the way his people worshipped and lived, hence the crucial role to be played by the Spirit.

The Spirit, promised as part of the new covenant, would produce the righteousness the former covenant called for but failed to produce. The Spirit has now been experienced by Jew and Gentile alike, and that quite apart from Torah. Thus the Spirit, as the eschatological fulfillment of the promised new covenant, plays a central role in Paul's argumentation whenever Gentile inclusion, Torah-free, is the issue.[4]

The Spirit Brings an End to Torah Observance

The gift of the Spirit as the new covenant *replacement* of Torah and the new covenant *fulfillment* of Torah's righteous requirement is the key to one of the nagging questions in our reading of Paul: How are we to understand his view of the law?[5] Our primary difficulty here stems from the tension we feel over many of Paul's own statements. He sometimes speaks of the law in a negative way, as having had its day; these stand side by side, sometimes in the same contexts, with other statements that affirm Torah as good and as being established by faith. Here as much as at any other place we face the complications of Paul's simultaneous continuity and discontinuity with the Old Testament.

On the one hand, Paul can speak of the law as bringing knowledge of sin (Rom 3:20; 7:7-12) or as "arousing sin" (7:5); indeed, it was "added so that the trespass might increase" (5:20). To be under the law is to be in prison, to be under slavery (Gal 3:23; 4:1); it means to be a descendant of Hagar rather than of Sarah (Gal 4:21-31). Having increased the transgression, it led to condemnation (2 Cor 3:9); and it was helpless to do anything about it (Rom 7:14-25; 8:3). For this reason the law ultimately deals in death, not life (2 Cor 3:6; Gal 2:19; Rom 7:5, 9). Those who promote Torah observance therefore belong to "the mutilation" (Phil 3:2); they are enemies of Christ whom Paul wishes would go the whole way and castrate themselves (Gal 5:12). With the coming of Christ and the Spirit, therefore, the time of Torah has come to an end (Rom 10:4; Gal 5:18, 23). All these passages clearly emphasize discontinuity.[6]

On the other hand, Paul sees the law as "holy" and "Spiritual" and its requirements as "holy, righteous, and good" (Rom 7:12, 14). The singular advantage of the Jews is that they have "been entrusted with the very words of God" (3:2; cf. 9:4); and to these words Paul appeals again and again as still having authority for God's people. Thus faith does not nullify the law; rather it establishes, or upholds, it (3:31). If circumcision is out, the same cannot be said of the commandments of God (1 Cor 7:19).

How, then, shall we reconcile such diversity? The traditional way was theological: the law as a means of achieving right standing with God has had its day, to be replaced by faith in Christ. But this view tends to read the Old Testament rather poorly, as though keeping the law were a means of gaining God's favor in the Old Testament. The authors of Psalms 19 and 119 surely did not think so!

The solution lies with the role of the Spirit in Paul's understanding. Indeed, the experience of the promised eschatological Spirit, not righteousness by faith, forms the core of Paul's argumentation in the one letter (Galatians) devoted primarily to this issue. The death of Christ brought an end to the curse of the law—that one had to live by "doing the law" and thus not "by faith" (Gal 3:10–14). The gift of the Spirit makes the law's function of identifying God's people obsolete. "Those who are led by the Spirit," Paul says, "are not under Torah" (5:18). For those in whom the fruit of the Spirit is growing "there is no law" (v. 23). For Paul the Spirit thus marks the effective end of Torah. How so? Because the Spirit is sufficient to do what Torah was not able to do in terms of righteousness, namely, to "*fulfill* in us who walk by the Spirit the righteous commandment of Torah" (Rom 8:4).

Herein lies the discontinuity and continuity. In the age of the Spirit, discontinuity lies in the area of Torah observance—keeping the law as a way either to identify the people of God or to establish one's relationship with God. Paul's break with his Jewish tradition at this point is absolute—and resolute: "Neither circumcision nor uncircumcision counts for anything; what counts is keeping the commandments of God" (1 Cor 7:19). Even though it counts for nothing, Jewish parents may continue to circumcise their sons if they wish, as long as they understand that it has no bearing on their being counted among the people of God. But also because it counts for nothing, one may not impose it on Gentiles, precisely because that would give it religious significance. Continuity lies in the Spirit's "fulfilling" Torah by leading God's people in the paths of God, to live in such a way so as to express the original intent of Torah: to create a people for God's name, who bear God's likeness in their character, as is seen in their behavior.

The fruit of the Spirit is none other than the Spirit's producing in our lives the righteousness of God (the righteousness that characterizes God). When this is happening Torah is fulfilled in such a way that for all practical purposes it has become obsolete; however, Torah as part of the Old Testament story, of which ours is the continuation, is never obsolete. In this sense it will endure as long as this between-the-times existence endures—not as a means of righteousness or as a means of identity, but as a means of pointing us to the righteousness of God, which the Spirit brings to pass in our lives in the present expression of the eschatological future.[7]

THE NATURE OF CHRISTIAN ETHICS

According to 1 Corinthians 7:19, while circumcision counts for nothing, "keeping the commandments of God" does count. Is Paul now bringing the law in again through the back door? Hardly. This is simply his way of saying that righteousness as an expression of God's character in his people's lives is not optional. The reason for this lies with the gift of the promised Spirit, who has both rendered Torah observance obsolete and made possible the fulfillment of the righteous requirement of Torah. The goal of Torah, God's own righteousness reflected in his people, is precisely what the Spirit can do, which Torah could not. Here is the crux of things regarding Spirit ethics. Only those matters which have to do with God and his character are regarded as absolute; all others are *adiaphora*, nonessentials.

The Spirit is central in Paul's ethics, first, because there is no such thing as "salvation in Christ" that does not also include righteousness on the part of God's people.

Paul's attitude toward these matters is clearly expressed in Romans 14:17, the theological insertion that lies at the heart of Paul's response to some practical ethical questions. How do those who follow certain religious practices live together as one people of God with those who do not, so that "together with one voice" they might "glorify the God and Father of our Lord Jesus Christ" (Rom 15:6)? Paul's answer is that the one who is observant must not condemn the nonobservant, and the nonobservant must not scorn the observant (14:1–6). The reason? "The kingdom of God has nothing at all to do with food and drink [utter nonessentials], but with the righteousness, joy, and peace that the Holy Spirit empowers" (14:17). Food and drink count for nothing; righteousness, joy, and peace count for everything.

Thus the Spirit is central in Paul's ethics, first, because there is no such thing as salvation in Christ that does not also include righteousness on the part of God's people. They are not saved by doing righteousness—that is unthinkable, since righteousness as behavior is the *product* of the Spirit's empowering, not a requirement of obedience in order to get in. But for that very reason ethical life is also required, because both getting in and staying in are the work of the Spirit, and Paul sees no division between the two.

Truly Christian ethics can only be by the Spirit's empowering.

Second, the Spirit is essential to Paul's ethics because truly Christian ethics can only be by the Spirit's empowering. That is why Torah observance does not work; it may make people "religious," but it fails to make them truly "righteous," in the sense of reproducing the righteousness of God in their lives. Spirit people not only *want* to please God but are *empowered* to do so.

This is also why Spirit ethics starts with a renewed mind (Rom 12:1–2; cf. Col 1:9; Eph 1:17), because only in this way may we determine what God's will is and thus be pleasing to him. The mind renewed by the Spirit leads us to understand that love must rule over all; and only by such a renewed mind may we discover how best to love. There is a time for speaking and a time for silence, a time for taking another's load on oneself and a time to refrain from that for the sake of the other's growth. Only dependence on the Spirit can enable us to know what is pleasing to God.

The passages in Colossians and Ephesians are especially significant in this regard. Although the specific nature and form of the Colossians' heresy to which Paul is responding may be shrouded in mystery for us, there can be little question that it included: (1) an appeal to something heady (wisdom, so-called philosophy, etc.), probably based on visions, and (2) an insistence on religious righteousness approaching an ascetic ideal ("don't touch, don't taste, don't handle"). Paul's response to this early on in the letter (Col 1:9–11) is to pray for the Colossian believers that they might "be filled with the knowledge of God's will by means of the Spirit's

wisdom and insight," and this precisely so that they might walk
worthy of the Lord in ways that are pleasing to him (cf. Rom
12:1–2).

Ethics for Paul,

therefore, is ultimately

a theological issue

pure and simple—that

is, an issue related to

the known character

of God.

Thus, rather than give them Christian rules to live by Paul gives them the Spirit. Through the Spirit's wisdom and insight they are to be done with rules and advance to living the life of those who by the Spirit are being "renewed into the likeness of the Creator" (Col 3:10). The Creator's character is then spelled out (v. 12) in language reminiscent of the fruit of the Spirit in Galatians 5:22–23. This is the new form of revelation, which comes through the Spirit, who reveals God's will in such a way that ethical life is a reflection of God's character.

Ethics for Paul, therefore, is ultimately a theological issue pure and simple—that is, an issue related to the known character of God. Everything has to do with God, and what God is about in Christ and the Spirit. Thus: (1) the *purpose* (or basis) of Christian ethics is the glory of God (1 Cor 10:31); (2) the *pattern* for such ethics is the Son of God, Christ himself (1 Cor 4:16–17; 11:1; Eph 4:20), into whose likeness we were predestined to be transformed (Rom 8:29); (3) the *principle* is love, precisely because love is at the essence of who God is;[8] (4) and the *power* is the Spirit, the Spirit of God.

Hence the essential role of the Spirit. Since the Spirit of God is the Spirit of Christ, and since the first-mentioned fruit of the Spirit is love, the Spirit not only empowers the believer for ethical behavior, but by indwelling the believer also reproduces the pattern and the principle of that behavior.

Walking in/by the Spirit[9]

The central role of the Spirit is most clearly spelled out in Galatians 5:13–6:10, where with a series of verbs modified by the phrase *pneumati* ("in/by the Spirit"), Paul urges the Galatians to "make a completion" (3:3) by means of the same Spirit by whom they had been converted. They are commanded to "walk in the Spirit," and promised that those who so walk "will not fulfill the desire of the flesh" (v. 16); such people are "led by the Spirit," attested by "the fruit of the Spirit" (vv. 22–23), and are not under Torah (vv. 18, 23). Since they "live by the Spirit" (= have been brought to life by the life-giving Spirit), they must also "behave in accordance with the Spirit" (v. 25). Finally, only those who "sow to the Spirit" in this way "will reap the *eternal* life" that is also from the Spirit (6:8).

Two things are clear from this passage: that the Spirit is the key to ethical life, and that Paul expects Spirit people to exhibit changed behavior. The first instruction, "walk by the Spirit," is the basic command in Paul's ethics. The verb "to walk" was commonly used in Judaism to refer to a person's whole way of life. Paul adopted it as his most common verb for ethical conduct (17 occurrences in all). All other commands proceed from this one. The primary form that such walking takes is "in love" (Eph 5:2; Gal 5:6), hence love is the first-mentioned "fruit of the Spirit" (Gal 5:22; cf. 5:14; Rom 13:8–10).

There are also some things that Spirit ethics is not in Paul's letters. On the one hand, Spirit ethics is not simply an ideal, to be achieved by those few who are truly "spiritual," as over against some who are still "carnal" or fleshly. The empowering of the Spirit belongs to all alike. Paul would have as little patience with a view that allows for people to be "justified sinners" without appropriate changes in attitudes and conduct (see ch. 7 above), as he would with an appeal to helplessness on the part of those who live in and walk by the Spirit (see ch. 11 below). Paul simply knows nothing about an internal struggle within the human breast, in which the flesh continually proves to be the greater power.[10] After all, Spirit ethics is not first of all a matter of individual piety, but of our life together in the world.

On the other hand, Spirit ethics is neither ethical perfectionism (life without sin at all) nor triumphalism (plastic smiles that convey perpetual victory in all circumstances). Life in the Spirit is ethical realism, life lived in the already/not yet by the power of the Spirit. If someone is overtaken in a trespass, the rest of God's Spirit people restore that person through the Spiritual fruit of gentleness (Gal 6:1–2). One who has brought grief to Paul and the community by his opposition to Paul is to be forgiven and thus restored (2 Cor 2:5–11).

The key for Paul lay with the Spirit as a dynamically experienced reality in the life of both believers (Gal 3:2, 4) and community (3:5).[11] Paul's expectation level was high on this matter because for him and his churches the Spirit was not simply believed in but was experienced in tangible, visible ways. If our experience of the Spirit lies at a lower level, we must resist the temptation to remake Paul into our image and thereby find comfort in a Paul that did not exist. Paul's answer was "walk in/by the Spirit," and he assumed that such a walk was available to those who had already "experienced so many things" of the Spirit (Gal 5:4). He does not tell us *how* to do that because such a dynamic life in the Spirit was presumed by him.

The Spirit as Holy[12]

Although Paul usually uses the term "sanctification" to refer to Christian conversion (see ch. 7 above), the word tends to appear where his concern is with his converts' improper (sinful) behavior.[13] For example, in 1 Thessalonians 4:3–8 he takes up the issue of sexual immorality with a group of former pagans for whom sexual irregularity was *not* considered a moral issue. Paul sees such conduct both as over against God and as wronging another believer. The argument begins, "this is God's will for you, even your sanctification" (v. 3), and concludes that the person who rejects Paul's instruction on this matter does not reject what a mere man has to say, "but rejects the very God who *gives* [present tense] you his *Holy* Spirit." This further explains the use of the word "sanctification" in reminding them of their conversion in 2 Thessalonians 2:13, as well as the repeated emphasis on sanctification in 1 Corinthians (see 1:2, 30; 6:11).

Here we see at least in part the significance of the early church's referring to the Spirit as the *Holy* Spirit. The early believers understood themselves to be dedicated to God, but not in a ritual way, as in the Old Testament use of the term "sanctified." Rather, they were set apart for God, to be his holy people in the world.[14] Hence the emphasis in 1 Thessalonians 4:3-8.

For Paul, "holiness," that is, walking by means of the *Holy* Spirit, has two aspects. On the one hand, it means abstaining from some sins— absolutely. Since in Christ believers have died to both sin (the flesh) and the law, they are to serve God "in the newness of the Spirit" (Rom 7:6). They must put to death the former way of life (Rom 6:1-18; 8:12-13; Col 3:5-11), portrayed in Galatians 5:19-21 as "the works of the flesh," which refers to life before and outside Christ. Such a life is no longer an option for the new people of God, who indeed have become a people by the indwelling of the Spirit of God. Paul, therefore, understands "putting to death" the works of the flesh as the empowering work of the Spirit (Rom 8:12-13).

> *"Holiness" also (especially) means the Holy Spirit living in believers, reproducing the life of Christ within and among them, particularly in their communal relationships.*

On the other hand, "holiness" also (especially) means the Holy Spirit living in believers, reproducing the life of Christ within and among them, particularly in their communal relationships. To do otherwise is to "grieve the Holy Spirit of God" (Eph 4:30), who by his presence has given them both unity and mutual growth. For this reason, Paul's most common language for the people of God is "the saints" (= God's *holy* people). They live differently in their relationships with one another, and are empowered to do so, because they are Spirit people, whatever else they may be.

What remains to be looked at in terms of Christian conversion is what the converted person looks like, how "holiness" is expressed in the life of the believing community. The answer to this question is taken up next; and again the Spirit, the renewed presence of God, is the key to our being transformed into God's own likeness.

NOTES

1. I should add, to fill out the debate at the popular level, that too much ranting against "eternal security" often led to insecurity. My way of putting it is that a lot of us used to "get saved" every Sunday night because we had sinned during the week! This equally bad theology led to more spiritual neuroses than one cares to remember.

2. On the question of Paul's ethics, see especially V. P. Furnish, *Theology and Ethics in Paul* (Nashville: Abingdon, 1968); for the role of the Spirit in Paul's ethics, see especially the perceptive paragraphs in E. Käsemann, *Commentary on Romans* (Grand Rapids: Eerdmans, 1980) 324-25. See also in *GEP* the discussion on 1 Thess 4:8; 2 Thess 2:13; 1 Cor 6:19-20; Gal 5:5-6, 13-15, 16-18, 19-23, 24-26; 6:1-3; Rom 6:1-8:39; 7:5-6, 14, 18; 8:1-2, 3-4, 5-8, 12-13; 13:11-14; 14:16-18; Eph 4:3-4, 30.

3. Among scores of such texts see, e.g., the powerful appeal of Isa 58.

4. See *GEP* on 2 Cor 3:1-4:6 (cf. 11:4); Gal 3:1-4:7; 4:29; 5:1-6, 13-24; Rom 7:4-6; 8:1-30; Phil 3:2-3.

5. For helpful introductions to the issues and the debate on Paul and the Law, see esp. S. Westerholm, *Israel's Law and the Church's Faith: Paul and his Recent Interpreters* (Grand Rapids: Eerdmans, 1988), and F. Thielman, *Paul and the Law: A Contextual Approach* (Downers Grove: InterVarsity Press, 1994).

6. Indeed, much of the literature on Paul and the law stems from the need to explain how a Jew like Paul could bear such un-Jewish sentiments toward Torah.

7. For the exegesis that leads to these various conclusions, see *GEP* on 2 Cor 3:1-18; 3:4-6, 7-11; Gal 3:1-5, 14; 4:4-7, 29; 5:5-6, 13-15, 18, 19-23; Rom 2:29; 7:5-6, 14, 18; 8:1-2, 3-4; 12:1-2; Phil 3:3.

8. The passages here are numerous: Gal 5:13-14; 1 Cor 8:2-3; 13:4-7; Rom 13:8-10; Col 3:14; Eph 5:2, 25.

9. See the discussion in *GEP* on Gal 5:13-6:10; 2 Cor 12:18; Col 1:9-11; Eph 4:1-3.

10. As we will discuss in ch. 11, the whole point of the argument of Gal 5:13-6:10 has to do with the adequacy of the Spirit for our righteousness, as we continue to live as Spirit people in a world where the perspective of the flesh is still the dominant force. The point of the command in Gal 5:16 is *promise*: "Walk by the Spirit, and you will not fulfill the desire of the flesh."

11. As noted in the analysis of Gal 5:16 in *GEP*, 427-34.

12. See the discussion in *GEP* on such diverse texts as 1 Thess 4:8; 2 Thess 1:11; 2:13; 1 Cor 6:11; Rom 15:16; Eph 4:30.

13. Except for instances where he is making a play on the new and old covenants, as in Rom 15:16. There his point has to do with formerly

unclean Gentiles now sanctified by the Spirit, so that they may not be judged by Jewish Christians for their lack of ritual purity, especially their rejection of circumcision and food laws.
14. Compare A. W. Wainwright, *The Trinity in the New Testament* (London: SPCK 1962) 22–23.

CONVERSION: STAYING IN (PART 2)—THE FRUIT OF THE SPIRIT

*The goal of individual conversion is for us to bear
the fruit of the Spirit, that is, to be transformed
into God's own likeness, the likeness of Christ.*

"You've come a long way, baby," the cigarette ad announces to
those women it is trying to seduce with its deadly product. The
implication is that smoking this brand will bring them "the whole
way" into the modern world. The ad, of course, has it all wrong,
desperately wrong, not only in its demeaning of women but also
in its implications about the goal of the journey. In the real
journey into the life of the future, we come a long way only as we
walk in the Spirit. Thus are we conformed more and more into the
likeness of God's Son, our Lord Jesus Christ.

To change metaphors: However much we may wish it otherwise, when we receive the Spirit at conversion divine perfection
does not set in, but divine "infection" does! We have been
invaded by the living God himself, in the person of his Spirit,
whose goal is to infect us thoroughly with God's own likeness.
Paul's phrase for this infection is the fruit of the Spirit. The
coming of the Spirit, with the renewing of our minds, gives us a
heavenly appetite for this fruit. The growing of this fruit is the
long way on the journey of Christian conversion, the "long
obedience in the same direction," and it is altogether the work of

the Spirit in our lives. Life at a lower level is no advertisement for the future!

My primary purpose in this chapter is to look more closely at Paul's list of these "fruit" in Galatians 5:22–23—a list that in effect is a mirror image of Christ himself, and thus also a reflection of what Spirit people look like. But before that, we take a brief look at how broad Paul's understanding of life in the Spirit really is.

OTHER SPIRIT ACTIVITY

All sorts of other activities besides ethical "fruit" are understood by Paul as the work of the Spirit. Most of these belong to the life of the individual believer. What they reveal is the wide range of Paul's view of life in Christ as empowered by the Spirit.[1]

Paul's view of life in Christ is so thoroughly dominated by the Spirit that the Spirit is the one absolutely essential ingredient for that life.

For example, our experience of hope—for the certain future noted in chapter 5 above—is empowered by the Spirit (Gal 5:5; Rom 15:13). Similarly, in Romans 9:1 Paul indicates that his clear conscience regarding what he is about to say is the work of the Spirit in his life. If Romans 12:11 refers to the Spirit at work in the believer's spirit, then the Spirit is also the source of zeal for service. In Philippians 1:19 Paul expects the combination of the Philippians' praying and the "supply of the Spirit" to make it possible for him to experience either deliverance or death without shaming the gospel, and to the glory of Christ. And even though he makes little of it with regard to apostleship, the Spirit is the key to Paul's "many visions and revelations" (2 Cor 12:1; see further ch. 12 below).

These several texts together merely demonstrate further what has already been said—that Paul's view of life in Christ is so thoroughly dominated by the Spirit that the Spirit is the one absolutely essential ingredient for that life. Our focus in this chapter, however, is with the ethical dimension of that life, as illustrated by the fruit of the Spirit.

THE SPIRIT AND HIS FRUIT

Before we look at the fruit individually, some general observations about the list of fruit in its context in Galatians might prove helpful.

1. Although Paul sets out the fruit of the Spirit in contrast to the preceding works of the flesh, he does not thereby intend passiveness on the part of the believer. After all, ethical instruction elsewhere comes by way of command, calling believers to active obedience. What we must not disregard is the element of the miraculous. In Paul's ethics we walk in the Spirit (Gal 5:16) as we are led by the Spirit (v. 18). The Spirit produces the fruit as believers continually walk with the Spirit's help.

2. The essential nature of the fruit is the reproduction of the life of Christ in the believer. As noted in chapter 3 above, the Spirit is in fact the Spirit of Christ. We are not surprised therefore that many of the words Paul uses to describe this fruit are used elsewhere of Christ. In Ephesians 4:20 he speaks of ethical life in terms of "learning Christ." The fruit of the Spirit is simply another way of talking about our being "predestined to be conformed to the likeness of God's Son" (Rom 8:29).

3. It is misleading to refer to this list as the ninefold fruit of the Spirit. The list is intended to be not exhaustive but representative, just like the preceding list of vices in Galatians 5:19–21. Paul concludes both lists by referring to "such things," meaning all other vices and virtues similar to these. All such lists, including the description of love in 1 Corinthians 13:4–7 and of *charismata* ("gifts of the Spirit") in 1 Corinthians 12:8–10, are written for the occasion and tailored to their contexts. In this case, they have been fashioned to address the conflict in the Galatian congregations (see Gal 5:15 and 26). This also means that a full discussion of the fruit of the Spirit would need to spread a wide net to include, for

example, the further items mentioned in Colossians 3:12-13 (compassion, humility, forgiveness) as well as specific applications like those in Romans 12:9-21.

4. These fruit cover a broad range, including all manner of attitudes, virtues, and behavior. Every aspect of Christian life, across the broadest possible spectrum, is the work of the Spirit. Fruit include the experiences of joy and peace within the believing community; attitudes such as gentleness, forbearance, and self-control; and behavior such as love, kindness, goodness, and all others consonant with these.

5. To reiterate from chapter 9 above, this list of Spiritual fruit is *not* intended to regulate Christian behavior by rules of conduct. Because truly Christian ethics are the product of walking and living in the Spirit, there can be no law (Gal 5:23); nor may we turn Paul's ethics into a new law. Rather these fruit are pointers; here is what one who is being conformed into Christ's image will look like.

6. To bring this discussion full circle, most of these items have to do not with the internal life of the individual believer but with the corporate life of the community. While it is true that individuals must love, work toward peace, express forbearance, kindness, and goodness, and be characterized by gentleness, in Pauline ethics these virtues characterize God's relationship toward his people. The Spirit bears fruit in our individual lives for the same purpose, to be toward one another the way God is toward us.

This is demonstrated in Galatians 6:1 by Paul's use of "the S/spirit of gentleness" as the motivation behind their restoration of a brother or sister who has sinned. When Paul admonishes in 6:4 that they are to "test" or "examine" themselves, that is not a call to introspection, Christian "navel gazing" as it were, but for them to see whether as individuals the fruit of the Spirit are at work in each of them for the sake of the common good.

Thus the opening command, "walk by the Spirit" (Gal 5:16), is directed not so much toward the individual in terms of his or her own personal life in Christ, but toward the Christian community, in which some are "biting and devouring" one another, hence using their freedom in Christ as an "occasion for the flesh." The flesh/Spirit contrast in this passage, therefore, has nothing to do with one's introspective conscience. It has everything to do with "love, joy, peace, forbearance, kindness, goodness, and gentleness" within the believing community. They are ethics for believers who are learning to live together as God's people in a fallen world.

THE INDIVIDUAL FRUIT

It is common to make more of the singular "fruit," in contrast to the plural "works," than the language will allow. Paul probably had no such contrast in mind, nor does he think of the works as many and individual but the fruit as one cluster with several kinds on it. The word *karpos* ("fruit") in Greek functions as a collective singular, much as the word "fruit" does in English. In both languages one would refer to "the fruit in the bowl," whether they are all of one kind or of several. Here they are of several kinds.

Love

That love should assume pride of place is no surprise. Paul has already accorded it such a place in this argument (Gal 5:6, 13–14), a place it always holds in his ethics,[2] as in all of Scripture. The reason for this is that in Paul's theology, resulting from his long life in the Old Testament, this word captures the essence of the character of God as seen in his relationship to his people.[3] Thus in the trinitarian benediction of 2 Corinthians 13:14, in which the primary characteristic of the divine Persons is expressed, Paul prays for the Corinthians to know "the love of God." God's love for his people is what has been poured out into their hearts by the Spirit (Rom 5:5). For Paul this love has been expressed most powerfully in God's sending his Son, and in the Son's death on the cross (Rom 5:6–8). God's love is full of forbearance and kindness (see below) toward his people, and finally expresses itself to the full in the self-sacrificial death of Christ on behalf of his enemies.

But for Paul this is not simply theory or abstract reality; the Spirit had poured this love into his heart. In this same letter he has already described the indwelling Christ as the one "who loved me and gave himself for me" (Gal 2:20). This is surely what he intends by the "law of Christ" in 6:2, which lies behind the imperative by which all of this began in 5:13 ("through love perform the duties of a slave for one another"). Such love is the direct result of being loved by the God whose love has been lavished on us in the Son, who likewise loved us and gave himself for us, and by whose indwelling presence we now live.

Love, therefore, is not something one can do or feel on one's own; nor is it to be distorted into its current North American version of good feelings toward someone, so that love is turned on its head—instead of self-sacrificial giving of myself for others, it has become identified with what I do or feel for another for the sake of my own self-fulfillment. Love heads this list of virtues over against the works of the flesh precisely because it stands as the stark opposite of the self-centeredness of most of the items on the former list. As the fruit of the Spirit, love spells the end to "hostilities, strife, jealousy, outbursts of rage, selfish ambitions, dissensions, factions, envies," and the like (see Gal 5:20–21). This can only be lived out in the context of other people, especially other believers. Thus it is Paul's own antidote in vv. 13 and 14 to their internal strife mentioned in v. 15.

> *Life in Christ, and therefore life by the Spirit, is a life of joy; above all else, such joy is to characterize the Christian community.*

Joy[4]

Life in Christ, and therefore life by the Spirit, is a life of joy; above all else, such joy is to characterize the Christian community (1 Thess 5:16). What is remarkable is the appearance of joy in this list of virtues that are primarily ethical in character. As with love and peace that stand on either side of it, Paul is probably not thinking so much of the personal, individual experience of joy—although as with this whole list, that can scarcely be excluded—but of the joy that characterizes a community who are walking in the Spirit.[5]

God has brought us eschatological salvation; the future has already made its appearance in the present; God's people have already tasted the life that is to be. Already they have received full pardon, full forgiveness; by the Spirit they cry out *Abba* to the God who has loved them and given his Son for them. This is cause for joy, unquenchable, uninhibited joy, as "by the Spirit we eagerly await the hope of righteousness" (Gal 5:5). The fruit of the Spirit is *joy*, joy in the Lord. What must begin at the individual level must also therefore characterize the believing community, among whom God still generously supplies the Holy Spirit.

The presence or absence of joy is therefore unrelated to one's circumstances, as Paul's letter to the Philippians makes plain. It is related entirely to what God has done for us in Christ through the Spirit. The Pauline imperative, stemming from joy as the fruit of the Spirit, is not simply "rejoice"—although it often comes in that simple form as well—but "rejoice *in the Lord.*" This focus is the key to our understanding the joy of the Spirit. A community that is "rejoicing *in the Lord* always" is not a community easily given to "eating and devouring one another" (Gal 5:15), one in which people think too highly of themselves (6:4).

Peace

As with love, peace is especially associated with God and his relationship to his people; and as with love and joy, for Paul it is especially a community matter. That is, Paul's first concern with peace is not the well-arranged heart—although again, it is difficult to have peace in a community where God's people themselves know little peace individually. But here peace occurs in a list of virtues that deliberately stand over against the works of the flesh, eight of which describe the causes or results of human discord.

God himself is often described as "the God of peace,"[6] the God who dwells in total *shalom* (wholeness, well-being) and who gives such *shalom* to his people in their life together. What is striking is that this divine ascription occurs exclusively in contexts where there is strife or unrest close at hand. Thus the antidote to unruly *charis-*

mata in the community is the theological note that God himself is a "God of peace" (1 Cor 14:33); or in a community where the unruly idle live off the largesse of others, Paul prays that the God of peace will give them peace at all times (2 Thess 3:16); or in a context where believers are warned against those who "cause divisions and put obstacles in your way," he assures them that the God of peace will bruise Satan under their feet shortly (Rom 16:20).

Furthermore, the mention of peace in Paul's letters (apart from the standard salutation) most often occurs in community or relational settings. Christ is our peace who has made Jew and Gentile one people, one body (Eph 2:14–17), who are urged to "keep the unity of the Spirit through the bond of peace" (4:3). Similarly in the argument of Romans 14:1–15:13, Paul urges Jew and Gentile together to "make every effort to do what leads to peace" (14:19). In the community context of Colossians 3:12–4:6, Paul urges the Colossians to "let the peace of Christ rule in your hearts, since as members of one body you were called to peace." Peace, therefore, has primarily to do with the cessation of hostilities. Blessed are the peacemakers! The Spirit alone can produce such peace in our midst.

Forbearance

It is common to translate this word (Greek *makrothymia*) as "patience." To be sure, in some cases it may well carry that meaning. But in English, patience tends to be individualistic; that is, one is patient about all kinds of nonpersonal matters pertaining to life in general (e.g., burnt toast). But in Paul *makrothymia* and its corresponding verb are always used in contexts involving one's forbearance toward others.[7] As such it often refers, as it does here, to the passive but tenacious side of love, of which its companion "kindness" is the active side. Thus Paul describes God's attitude toward human arrogance as one of forbearance and kindness (Rom 2:4). These are the first two words that describe (God's) love in 1 Corinthians 13:4; and they occur together in Colossians 3:12 as part of Christian dress when we "put on Christ."

Thus "longsuffering" (KJV) has to do with long forbearance toward those who stand over against us in some way. Although Paul nowhere else attributes such forbearance to the direct working of the Spirit, its appearance here makes clear that Spirit empowering is not simply for joy and miracles, but also for this much-needed quality of hanging in there with those who need long and patient love and kindness (cf. Col 1:11). This is the antidote to "outbursts of rage" (5:20) or "provoking one another" (v. 26).

Kindness

Like the forbearance with which it is frequently allied, the key to understanding "kindness" is found in the instances where it describes God's character or activity toward people. Thus it occurs as a verb in 1 Corinthians 13:4 to express the active side of love, for which longsuffering expresses its passive side. In such a context it surely refers to God's active goodness, lavished upon those whom he loves. God's kindness is found in his thousandfold acts of mercy toward people like ourselves who deserve his wrath. This is especially borne out by its usage in Ephesians 2:7, where the extravagant expression of God's grace is demonstrated in his kindness toward us in Christ.

In this list, of course, where it occurs again in conjunction with forbearance, it has to do with genuine acts of kindness toward others. As such it fits the larger context as another contrast to the works of the flesh, with their self-centered, basically hostile-toward-others way of life. The Spirit not only empowers us to endure the hostility or unkindness of others; he also enables us to show kindness to them, actively to pursue their good. If longsuffering means not to "chew someone's head off" (see Gal 5:15), kindness means to find ways of binding up their wounds.

Goodness

As noted above, this word is closely allied with kindness. If there is a difference, "goodness" is the more all-embracing quality, describing one's character. The adjective ("good") from which this noun is formed is a primary word to describe God's character in the Old Testament. Similarly, believers may be described as "full of goodness" (Rom 15:14); when put into practice it takes the form of "doing good." Indeed, goodness does not exist apart from its active, concrete expression.

Thus this is the quality of Christian grace, produced in the life of the believer by the Spirit, that Paul picks up on at the end to conclude the present argument: "let us do good to all people" (Gal 6:9–10). Again, as with the preceding words, its appearance here presupposes the present context. Those who sow to the Spirit are those who do good to all; obviously this stands as yet another antonym to those works of the flesh that have found a measure of existence among the Galatians.

Faith(fulness)

The word here is *pistis*, Paul's primary word for "faith," having to do with one's basic stance toward God—of utter trust in his trust-worthiness. In the Septuagint it was the basic Greek word used for the concept of *God's* faithfulness. This is the sense that Paul picks up in Romans 3:3, that the "unfaithfulness" of God's people does not call into question God's own *pistis* ("faithfulness"). From a theological perspective, one could not object to faith as the meaning of the word even here—that is, that one of the fruit of the Spirit is our trust in God. But given the other virtues, especially those that immediately surround it, Paul is no doubt referring to faithfulness, that is, our faithful living out our trust in God over the long haul.

The more difficult question is whether it also carries a nuance of faithfulness in relationship to others. Since the New Testament has no other examples of such usage, it seems unlikely, despite the context, that Paul has this nuance in mind here. More likely the sense is that of faithful devotion to God, which in turn will express itself toward others by means of the various other fruit in this list. True faith for Paul always includes the element of faithfulness; thus true faith for him in this sense, as a fruit of the Spirit, expresses itself in love (Gal 5:6).

Gentleness

This is the word that earlier versions translated "meekness." For Paul it derives its Christian meaning from its relationship with

Christ. In Matthew 11:25–30 this is one of the two words used to describe the character of Christ, which he, as the only Son of the Father, revealed about the character of the Father. That Paul knew this tradition, or one like it, seems certain from his appeal to the "meekness and gentleness of Christ" in 2 Corinthians 10:1.

As a Christian grace, reflecting the character of Christ himself, it occurs eight times in Paul.[8] This fruit is the most difficult to translate adequately by an English word. It conveys at least the sense of humility toward oneself (that is, a proper estimation of oneself before God) and considerateness toward others. It is to this fruit that Paul will appeal in Galatians 6:1, when he urges those who walk by the Spirit to restore a brother or sister overtaken in a fault. We need to do so in the "S/spirit of gentleness" both because the life of the other person is at stake, and because we thereby remember our own frailties and susceptibility to temptation. In this list it stands as the exact antonym to the work of the flesh translated "selfish ambition." It is that fruit of the Spirit at work in those who do not think too highly of themselves (6:3), but who "in humility consider others better than themselves" (Phil 2:3)—in the sense that their needs and concerns are to be looked after before one's own.

Self-Control

The last word on this list is unique in several ways. First, it is the one word on the list that does not appear elsewhere in Scripture with reference to the character of God. Second, the noun occurs only here in Paul's letters, although the verb occurs in 1 Corinthians 7:9 with reference to sexual continence and in 1 Corinthians 9:25 with regard to the self-discipline of the athlete.[9] Third, it is the one virtue in the list that is clearly aimed at the individual believer. This is not something one does in community; it is a general stance toward excesses of various kinds.

In contrast to the rest of the terms in the list, which take aim at those eight works of the flesh that have to do with relational breakdowns, this one takes aim at either (or both) the sexual indulgences that appear as the first three works of the flesh (sexual immorality, impurity, debauchery) or (and) the excesses with which that list concludes (drunkenness, orgies). This, too, is the effective working of the Spirit in the life of the believer.

In terms of Pauline ethics, we may not turn "self-control" into abstinence as such. Paul denounces anything that even smacks of abstinence per se as a Christian virtue (see 1 Cor 10:31–33; Rom 14:1–23; 1 Tim 4:1–5), for example, "don't handle, don't taste, don't touch" (Col 2:21). Because of this fruit of the Spirit, we are free to abstain from anything for the sake of others; but we may never turn such free giving up of food or drink or whatever into some virtue on its own. These are merely "human traditions," as Paul calls them (Col 2:22), the "teachings of demons" (1 Tim 4:2). Only the Spirit can set us free for self-control— life in moderation, but with abstention for the sake of someone else.

The need for Torah to "hem in human conduct because of the transgressions" (Gal 3:19, 22) has come to an end with the advent of the Spirit, God's own way of fulfilling the promised new covenant.

Paul concludes this list by bringing it back into context: "Against such things as these there is no law." This means something like, "when these virtues are evident among us because of the presence of the Spirit, Torah is an irrelevancy." There is no need of Torah to say to people who by the Spirit are loving one another, "you shall not kill," nor to say to those who are actively pursuing the good of others out of kindness, "don't covet."

This does not mean that reminders like this list are irrelevant— Paul himself is long on such—but that the need for Torah to "hem in human conduct because of the transgressions" (Gal 3:19, 22) has come to an end with the advent of the Spirit, God's own way of fulfilling the promised new covenant. This is Torah being etched on the heart, so that God's people will obey him (Jer 31:33; Ezek 36:27). Here also is the clear evidence that for Paul the elimination of Torah does not mean the end of righteousness. To the contrary, the Spirit produces the real thing, the righteousness of God himself, so that his children reflect his likeness.

Of equal importance, these are the fruit of the eschatological Spirit. In us and in our believing communities the Spirit is at work reproducing the very life of God, so that in our present between-the-times existence, we might live the life of the future, toward which we are walking. This is what lies behind Paul's command in Philippians 1:27, where in a wordplay on the fact that Philippi was a Roman colony, whose free people were therefore citizens of Rome, Paul urges them "to live out their [heavenly] citizenship in Philippi in a manner worthy of the gospel of Christ." Picking up this same imagery again in 3:20 he says that "our citizenship is in heaven."

God's people in Philippi were in effect a "colony of heaven" in this colony of Rome. Paul's point is that if people are to see what heaven is to be like, they should see it now in the way the heavenly citizens live their life together. Obviously, only the Spirit of the living God can pull that off! But that is what it is all about.

We need, finally, to return to the beginning. Pauline ethics has to do with walking—putting one foot in front of the other, if you will—and doing so in the Spirit, as we are led by the Spirit. Both Paul's exhortation to the community in Ephesians 5:18 ("be filled with the Spirit") and his instruction to Timothy in 2 Timothy 1:6–7 ("fan the gift into flame") imply the need for a continual, ongoing appropriation. The Spirit's presence is the crucial matter, but that presence does not automatically ensure a quickened, fervent Spiritual life. Both individuals and the church as a whole are exhorted to keep the gift aflame. One way of doing this is by mutual encouragement and growth in the context of community life, especially in worship (see chapter 13 below).

But before that, two further areas of life in the Spirit call for special attention, the Spirit/flesh and power/weakness contrasts. Most Christians see both of these as belonging to individual Christian life; but as has already been suggested in this chapter, that is simply not true of the former, at least not in Paul's view. To this matter we now turn.

NOTES

1. For the exegetical details in support of what is said about the following texts, see appropriate sections in *GEP*.

2. See, e.g., 1 Thess 3:12; 4:9–11; 1 Cor 13:1–13; 16:14; Rom 13:8–10; Col 3:14; Eph 5:2.

3. See, e.g., the key texts in Deut 7:7–8 and 10:15, a theme picked up in the prophets (Hos 3:1; 11:1; Isa 41:8; 43:4; 48:14; 60:10; 63:9), where the translators of the Septuagint used the Greek word *agapē*. As with many such words, this background in the Septuagint, not its classical or Hellenistic usage, tends to determine Pauline usage.

4. Beginning with this virtue, our tendency is to read this list as though it were first of all a description of personal piety; thus we most often use it as a kind of checklist to see how we are doing. I would not hereby argue against such a reading of the text; my concern is that in context Paul probably intended all of these as virtues that should characterize the life of the Christian community, as it lives out its corporate life with one another in the world.

5. One wonders whether the general lack of joy that characterizes much of contemporary North American Christianity suggests that the life of the Spirit has been generally downplayed in the interest of a more heady or performance-oriented brand of faith.

6. See 1 Thess 5:23; 2 Thess 3:16; 1 Cor 14:33; 2 Cor 13:11; Rom 15:33; 16:20; Phil 4:9.

7. The KJV translated it "longsuffering." It is still hard to improve on the KJV in 1 Cor 13:4, "Love suffereth long, and is kind."

8. 1 Cor 4:21; Gal 5:23; 6:1; Col 3:12; Eph 4:2; 1 Tim 6:11; 2 Tim 2:25; Titus 3:2.

9. The adjective also occurs in the list of virtues required of an overseer in Titus 1:8.

THE ONGOING WARFARE—THE SPIRIT AGAINST THE FLESH

*The Spirit–flesh conflict in Paul has to do not with
an internal conflict in one's soul, but with the
people of God living the life of the future
in a world where the flesh is still very active.*

A good friend wrote recently, "Christians seem to me to divide into two groups these days: the first lot don't think that sin matters very much anyway, and the second know perfectly well that it does, but still can't kick the habit."[1] This chapter picks up the concern of the second lot. Indeed, we now come to the real world! Painfully, for many of God's people the subject of this chapter tells the story of their Christian life, a story of ongoing inner conflict of soul. They take some comfort in believing that Paul was their companion in this struggle. If Paul, the great apostle of the faith, could write, "what I want to do I do not do, but what I hate I do" (Rom 7:15), then what hope is there for us? So they simply resign themselves to the struggle.

People come by this comfort by reading Galatians 5:17, the single Pauline text that speaks about a *conflict* between the Spirit and the flesh, in light of Romans 7:14–25—although the Spirit is not so much as mentioned in the Romans passage, where Paul describes the conflict that goes on in the soul of a person living under law and without the Spirit's help. People accept this unfortunate reading of Paul at face value, because the text in Romans vividly describes something they know only too well. Sadly, for the vast majority of those who adopt such a view, the flesh usually wins. Thus Paul's passion, namely, the sufficiency of the Spirit for all of life in the present age, is brushed aside as unrealistic in favor of one's own personal reality.

To be sure, such war does rage in the hearts of many. Often the warfare—and the sense of helplessness to live above it—is the direct result of the intense individualism of Western culture. Both secular psychology and much Christian teaching focus on the inner self: How am I doing according to some set of criteria for wholeness? Focused on the inner struggle, we can scarcely see Christ or walk confidently in the way of the Spirit. Instead of living out the fruit of the Spirit, in constant thankfulness for what the Spirit is doing in our lives and in the lives of others, our individualistic faith turns sourly narcissistic—aware of our personal failures before God, frustrated at our imperfections, feigning the love, joy, peace, and gentleness we wish were real. Our turmoil crowds out openness to the Spirit himself. In such spiritual malaise God almost always gets the blame.

But as real as this is for some, Paul is not addressing this issue when in Galatians 5:17 he speaks of the Spirit and "flesh" as in utter opposition to each other. Indeed, he would not even understand it. His world is that of Psalm 19, not that of "the introspective conscience of the West."[2] In consecutive verses (12–13), the psalmist acknowledges first his "errors" and "hidden faults" and then the possibility of "willful sins." The former is an acknowledgment of the depth of our fallenness; for these "hidden faults" he asks forgiveness. His concern—and it does not take the form of a struggle—is with the "willful sins." About these he prays that they will "not rule over me."[3] Paul's view is similar. In Galatians 5:17 he is not addressing a struggle over "hidden faults" but open disobedience to God in the form of "willful sins."

At issue for us in this chapter, therefore, is Paul's own view of the conflict between the Spirit and the flesh, between living *kata sarka* ("according to the flesh") and *kata pneuma* ("according to the Spirit"). Every occurrence of these terms in Paul has to do with our present eschatological existence—what it means for believers to live *together as a people,* defined by the already/not yet fulfillment of God's promises, in contrast to a former life defined and determined by the world. My point: Nowhere does Paul describe Christian life, life in the Spirit, as one of constant struggle with the flesh.[4] He simply does not speak to that question. His point rather is the sufficiency of the Spirit for God's new end-time people.

> *Nowhere does Paul describe Christian life, life in the Spirit, as one of constant struggle with the flesh.*

Basic to Paul's view is that, as with Torah observance, the time of the flesh is over for followers of Christ. According to Romans 7:4–6, Christ and the Spirit have, with the new covenant, brought an end to the time of the law and the flesh, which belong to our existence *before* and *outside* Christ. Continuing to live this way is incompatible with life "according to the Spirit" (Rom 8:5–8). But Paul's view does not represent triumphalism, as though people who lived by the Spirit were never tempted by the old life in the flesh or that they never succumbed to such. They have, and they do; and there is forgiveness for such, and gracious restoration.

A careful analysis of the key texts Galatians 5:17 and Romans 7:14–25 demonstrates that this is Paul's perspective. But we will be helped in that analysis by looking first at Paul's use of the term "flesh."[5]

THE MEANING OF "FLESH" IN PAUL

The place to begin such a study is with the Old Testament, since Paul's usage originates there. The Hebrew word *bāśār* refers primarily to the flesh of bodies, and by derivation sometimes to the bodies themselves. On a few occasions the term is extended to describe human frailty and creatureliness, usually in contrast to God as creator. Thus a common expression for all living beings, especially humans, is "all flesh," meaning "every creature." When the psalmist asks in light of his trust in God, "What can flesh do to me?" (Ps 56:4), he means that with God as his protector what can a mere human do to him (cf. Jer 17:5). In his anguish Job asks God, "Do you have eyes of flesh? Do you see as humans see?" While "flesh" is not a neutral term when used in this way, neither does it express a negative moral judgment; rather, it expresses the frailty of human creatureliness. It would be unthinkable to the Hebrew that sin lay in the flesh, since sin's origins lie in the human heart.

Although Paul rarely uses the Greek term *sarx* in its basic sense, as referring to the physical body, he regularly uses it in the extended sense as referring to our humanity in some way or another. Thus he can speak of "Israel according to the flesh" (1 Cor 10:18), or Abraham as our forefather "according to the flesh" (Rom 4:1), or of Jesus as descended from David "according to the flesh" (Rom 1:3), meaning in each case "according to ordinary human descent." In the same mode Paul recognizes present human life as still "in the flesh" (e.g., Gal 2:20; 2 Cor 10:3), that is, lived out in the present human body, characterized by frailty as it is.

Paul also uses *sarx*, however, in a more unusual sense, derived in part from intertestamental Judaism, but marked by his own basically eschatological view of life in the world. "Flesh" for him denotes humanity not simply in its creatureliness vis-à-vis God, but in its *fallen* creatureliness as utterly hostile to God in every imaginable way. It is in this sense that he contrasts life "according to the flesh" over against life "according to the Spirit." The one describes the present evil age in terms of human fallenness, where by nature each has turned to his or her own way; the other describes the eschatological age that has dawned with the coming of Christ and the Spirit, as described in chapter 5 above.

This does not make *sarx* an easy term to translate. The NIV often uses "sinful nature."[6] That translation works well in Romans 7, where Paul is describing the failure of his former life under the law. The "flesh" represents "another law in his members" that rises up to defeat the law of God and thus to render the law helpless. That "other law" is his own "sinful nature." But this rendering does not work well in other places, where he is describing what characterizes the whole world in its present fallenness.

The clearest instance in which Paul plays on the two basic senses of this word ("human frailty" and "human fallenness") is in 2 Corinthians 10:2–4. Accused by them of acting "according to the flesh" in the morally negative sense, Paul allows, for the sake of his argument, that he does indeed live "*in* the flesh," by which he means "in the weaknesses and limitations of present mortality." But, he goes on, I do not engage in warfare "*according to* the flesh," in keeping with the fallenness which characterizes the present age that, because of the cross and resurrection, is on its way out. This argument does not work at all if "flesh" is morally negative in both instances.

Our interest lies strictly with this latter sense, human fallenness, which has completely lost its relationship to the physical and has become strictly eschatological—and morally negative—describing existence from the perspective of those who do not know Christ, who thus live as God's enemies. It describes believers only *before* they came to be in Christ and live by the Spirit. Any conflict in this matter has to do with believers in Christ, people of the Spirit, continuing to behave according to their pre-Christ perspective and values. Paul's point always is, "Stop it." "Put off your old self," he says, and "put on the new self" (Eph 4:22, 24). My point, then, is that whenever "flesh" occurs in contrast to the Spirit, it always bears this eschatological sense.

THE SPIRIT-FLESH CONTRAST IN PAUL[7]

That Paul viewed the flesh as belonging to the past for believers, in the same way as he viewed Torah observance, is specifically stated in Romans 7:4–6: "When we *were* living in the flesh, the passions of sin, aroused by the law, *were* [also] at work in us; . . . but now, by dying to what once bound us, we have been set free . . . to walk in the new way of the Spirit." How Paul understands this is set forth vividly in 2 Corinthians 5:14–17:

> For Christ's love compels us, because we are convinced that one died for all, and therefore all died. And he died for all, that those who live should no longer live for themselves but for him who died for them

and was raised again. So then, from now on we regard no one from the perspective of the flesh. If indeed we once considered even Christ from this perspective, now we know him in this way no longer. So then, if anyone is in Christ, a new creation; the old things have passed away; behold, the new have come.

The death and resurrection of Christ and the gift of the Spirit have changed everything. The former order of things is described in terms of flesh, that basically self-centered, creature-oriented point of view, which has caused the Corinthians to regard Paul as he had formerly regarded Christ, as weak and therefore not of God. The flesh perceives things from the old age point of view, where value and significance lie in power, influence, wealth, and wisdom (cf. 1 Cor 1:26–31).

To be sure, such a worldview is still about. But for those in Christ, all of that has passed away; behold, the new has come, the time of the Spirit, in which there has been a total change in the definition of what has value or significance. The new model is the cross: the power lies not in externals but in the Spirit, who indwells believers and by grace is renewing the "inner person" (2 Cor 4:16), transforming us into God's own likeness (ultimately portrayed in Christ through the cross).

This eschatological view of the Spirit/flesh contrast is found in other passages as well:

1. "I could not speak to you as Spiritual, but as fleshly," Paul tells the Corinthians (1 Cor 3:1). The irony of this sentence lies in the fact that the Corinthians, who think of themselves as Spirit people, are thinking just as they did before they met Christ, just like those leaders of this passing age, who crucified Christ (2:6–8). Their attitude toward Paul's suffering and his message of the cross in effect makes them bedfellows with those who killed Christ, viewing things from the perspective of the flesh.

This is obviously eschatological terminology. Moreover, it does not reflect some internal struggle in the believer between these two kinds of existence. On the contrary, it describes the essential characteristics of the two ages, which exist side by side in unrelieved opposition in our present already but not yet existence. The one, flesh, has been condemned and is on its way out; they are to be done with that. Paul is cajoling them to live the real life of the Spirit.

2. Similarly, in Philippians 3:3 Paul warns against those who would insist on circumcision. He describes believers as those who serve "by the Spirit of God" and who put no confidence in "the flesh." Here "flesh" refers to self-confidence based on a presumed advantaged relationship with God evidenced by circumcision. But as noted in chapter 9 above, the Spirit also stands opposed to, by fulfillment, any form of Torah observance. Thus these too are basically eschatological realities. To revert to circumcision, that is, to put "confidence in the flesh," is to go back to the way that has come to an end with the death and resurrection of Christ and the gift of the Spirit.

3. The strong contrasts in Romans 8:5–8 likewise do not deal with internal conflict. Paul is again describing the two kinds of existence, and indicating their utter incompatibility. Those who walk according to the flesh—and it is clear in context that this does *not* mean believers, but those still outside Christ—"have their minds set on what the flesh desires" (v. 5). Such a mind-set is hostile to God, does not—indeed, cannot—submit to God's law, cannot please God (how in the world could it?), and ends up in death. That simply does not describe Christian life, not in Paul and not anywhere else.

Life in the Spirit is not just a stroll in the park.

The people of God, who walk according to the Spirit, live in bold contrast to flesh-walkers. Their minds are set on the things of the Spirit (their minds have been renewed by the Spirit, after all); in place of hostility to God, they live in peace; and instead of death, they know life.

That this is the conflict Paul describes is made certain in Romans 8:9, where he addresses his Christian readers: "but *you*," he says, "are *not in the flesh* [in the sense that the flesh-walkers in vv. 7–8 are], but in the Spirit [a whole new way of existence], since indeed the Spirit of God dwells in you."

But Paul also recognizes that life in the Spirit is not just a stroll in the park. So in Romans 8:12–13 he applies all of vv. 1–11 to their lives, by reminding them that by the Spirit they must continue to kill that to which they have already died (the already/not yet again). They were formerly controlled by, and thus under obligation to, the flesh. Their new obligation is to the Spirit, to walk in his ways, led by him (v. 14).

Life in the Spirit is not passive; nor is obedience automatic. We continue to live in the real world; we are, after all, both already and not yet. Therefore, the imperative for the already is walk in/by the Spirit. That assumes that we live in a world very much controlled by the flesh; but it also assumes that we now live in that world as different people, led by the Spirit and empowered by the Spirit to produce the fruit of righteousness, rather than to continue in the works of the flesh.

That leads us finally to Galatians 5:17 and Romans 7:13-25. We begin with the latter, since it does not have to do with this contrast at all; and conclude by another look at the Galatians passage (see ch. 10 above).

THE STRUGGLE IN ROMANS 7:13–25

What about the intense, deeply emotional narration of Paul's own internal conflict in Romans 7:13-25? Doesn't this passage suggest that Paul himself, even though a man of the Spirit, continually struggled in his inner person with the pull of the flesh? At first glance, and taking the passage out of context, one might think so. But three things reveal otherwise: the surrounding context, what Paul actually says, and what he does not say.

The context throughout has to do with the place of Torah in the Christian life. In vv. 1-6 Paul has made it clear, by repeating himself yet one more time, that the believer has no relationship to it at all. In the death of Christ we have died with respect to the law (v. 4). Not only so, he adds, but we have also died with respect to the flesh (vv. 5-6; note the past tense, "when we *were* in the flesh"). But Paul is also aware that he has been extremely hard on the law in his argument to this point, which will hardly sit well with his readers who are Jewish Christians. Besides, he does not really consider the law a bad thing—quite the contrary. His problem with the law was with its inadequacy, its helplessness to empower what it required.

So in vv. 7–25, he sets out to exonerate the law from any suggestion that, because it was implicated in our death, the law itself was a bad thing. To make this point, he argues in two ways. First, he says in vv. 7–12, what killed "me" (and "me" in this paragraph stands for all other Jews as well as for himself) was not the law but the innate sinfulness that the law aroused. The law is implicated in his "death," to be sure, but as an abettor, not as a direct cause.

This, too, could put the law in a bad light, so he starts all over again (v. 13), this time insisting that the law is not really to blame at all. Its fault lay in its helplessness to do anything about the sin it has aroused in us by making us vividly aware of sin's utter "sinfulness." This is said with great intensity, and in a way in which all who try to please God on the basis of law can empathize. In the final analysis it is a totally useless struggle. For the person under law, who has not experienced the gift of the Spirit, sin and the flesh are simply the stronger powers.

Enter Christ and the Spirit (Rom 8), as God's response to the anguished cry of 7:24. Not only is there no condemnation in Christ (that is, the judgment we all so richly deserve has been put into our past through the death of Christ), but we now live by a new "law," that of the Spirit of life (8:2). What the law was unable to do, Christ has now done for us (positionally) and the Spirit "fulfills" in us (experientially) as we "walk in the Spirit" (vv. 3–4).

Three simple points, then, in conclusion:

1. What Paul describes throughout is what it was like to live under the law; and whatever else is true of the Christian Paul, he did not consider himself to be under the law. What he describes, from his now Christian perspective, is what it was like to live under law before Christ and the Spirit. The use of "I" and the present tense of the verbs only heighten the intensity of his feelings toward the utter helplessness of the law to do anything about the real problem of sin.

2. The person here described never wins. Being under the helpless law, in the face of the more powerful flesh and sin, means to be sold as a slave under sin, and thus incapable of doing the good thing the law demands. Such a description is absolutely incompatible with Paul's view of life in Christ, empowered by the Spirit.

3. There is not a single mention of the Spirit in the entire passage (vv. 7–25). The Spirit was last mentioned in v. 6, as the key to our new life in Christ, who has brought our relationship with the law and the flesh to an end. Christ and the Spirit are then picked up again in 8:1–2 as the divine response to the anguished cry of the person struggling with sin, but with the helpless law standing by, pointing out the sinfulness of our sin, unable to do anything about it.

Thus the only questions Paul himself raises in this entire passage have to do with Torah, whether it is good or evil, and, once this is affirmed as good, how this good thing is still implicated in our death. Life under Torah alone is under scrutiny.

GALATIANS 5:17 IN CONTEXT

But what of Galatians 5:17, where Paul says (literally), "for the flesh has desires over against the Spirit, and the Spirit over against the flesh; for these two [realities] are in opposition to each other, so that whatever things you may wish [= feel like doing], these things you may not do"? Does this not indicate that there is an internal struggle of the Spirit against the flesh? In context, not so. In fact, this text is precisely in keeping with the texts previously looked at, where this contrast appears.

Verse 17 comes at the heart of an argument dealing with one urgent question: Since Torah observance is now a thing of the past because of the coming of Christ and the Spirit, what is to ensure righteousness? That is, Paul is arguing against (perhaps anticipating) Jewish Christian opposition that would see his bypassing Torah observance as a sure invitation to license and ungodliness. Indeed, as Romans 3:7–8 makes clear and Romans 6:1 implies, Paul has been charged with this very thing.

Paul takes up this question, typically, not in terms of the individual believer in a one-on-one relationship with God, but at the very point where the Galatians are living as they used to, when the flesh held sway. Paul therefore warns the Galatians not to let their new freedom in Christ serve as a base of operations for the flesh

(5:13), meaning in this case to continue to engage in strife within the community of faith (v. 15). Rather, in love they are to "perform the duties of a slave to one another" (v. 13). For love like this "fulfills the law" (v. 14).

Paul's response to vv. 13 and 15 is vv. 16–26. He begins in v. 16 with the basic imperative—and promise. "Walk in the Spirit," he urges them, "and you will not carry out the desire of the flesh."

He cares especially that the way God's people live provides a radical alternative to the world around them.

Since this responds to v. 15, he is not talking about the inner life of the believers, but of giving in to ungodly behavior within the community. After all, the works of the flesh that follow, all have to do with behavior, and eight of the fifteen items mentioned are sins of discord within the believing community.

Verse 17 functions to elaborate v. 16, and does so by way of what has been said in vv. 13–15. The elaboration simply says what we have seen him say elsewhere: walking in the Spirit is incompatible with life according to the flesh, because these two are in utter opposition to one another. And because they are utterly incompatible, those who live in the Spirit may not do whatever they please, that is, their new freedom in Christ does not permit them to continue living as they used to, by eating and devouring one another.

Thus the flesh-Spirit contrast has to do with those who have entered the new way of life brought about by Christ and the Spirit; Paul is urging them to live this way by the power of the Spirit. His point is that the Spirit stands in opposition to the other way of living, and is fully capable of empowering one to live so. It is not that Paul does not care about the inner life; he does indeed. But here he cares especially that the way God's people live provide a radical alternative to the world around them. Those who so walk by the Spirit will not keep on destroying the Christian community through strife and conflict.

In all the passages where Paul sets the Spirit against the flesh he insists that through the death of Christ and the gift of the Spirit, the flesh has been mortally wounded—killed, in his language. It is not possible, therefore, that from Paul's perspective a Spirit person would be living in such a way that she or he is sold as a slave to sin, who is unable to do the good she or he wants to do because of being held prisoner to the law of sin.

We live in the flesh, only in the sense of living in the present body of humiliation, subject to the realities of the present age; but we do not walk according to the flesh.

Believers live between the times. The already mortally wounded flesh will be finally brought to its end at the coming of Christ. The Spirit, already a present possession, will be fully realized at the same coming. To the degree that the old age has not yet passed away, we still must learn to walk by the Spirit, to behave in keeping with the Spirit, and to sow to the Spirit. We can do so precisely because the Spirit is sufficient. In Paul's view, we live in the flesh, only in the sense of living in the present body of humiliation, subject to the realities of the present age; but we do not walk according to the flesh. Such a way of life belongs to the past, and those who live that way are outside Christ and "shall not inherit the [final eschatological] kingdom of God" (Gal 5:21).

Paul is always a realist. The "new righteousness" that fulfills Torah, effected by the Spirit, is itself both already and not yet. To return to the preceding chapter, the coming of the Spirit means that "divine infection," not divine perfection, has set in. Our lives are now led by the one responsible for inspiring the law in the first place. But that does not mean that God's people cannot still be "overtaken in a fault" (Gal 6:1). The resolution of such between-the-times trespassing of God's righteous requirement is for the rest of God's Spirit people to restore such a one through the Spirit's gentleness. It means regularly to experience God's forgiveness and grace. It does *not* mean to accept constantly living in willful sin as inevitable, like a slow leak deflating our lives, as though the Spirit were not sufficient for life in the present.

———

If this explanation does not satisfy those of you who live in a constant struggle with some besetting sin, my word to you is to take heart from the gospel. I do not minimize the struggle. But you are loved by God, and that love has been "shed abroad in your heart by the Spirit." The key to life in the Spirit for some is to spend much more quiet time in thanksgiving and praise for what God has done—and is doing, and promises to do—and less time on intro-spection, focused on your failure to match up to the law.

Whenever you do feel like getting even for what someone has done to you rather than forgiving them as Christ has forgiven you, you are made to realize once more that you do still live between the times, between the time the infection set in and the perfection will be realized (see above, p. 112). But by the Spirit's leading, neither do you do whatever you wish—tear into somebody for what they have done to you—as you used to do without thinking. The Spirit, God's own presence—his *empowering* presence—is within, and will lead you into appropriate responses.

Finally, to bring this discussion full circle, here is where your being a member of the body comes in. Since the ultimate goal of salvation is for us individually to belong as a growing, contribut-ing, edifying member of the people of God, others in the body exist for the same purpose, and thus should serve you in the same way. Don't try to be a lone ranger Christian, slugging it out on your own. Seek out those in the community to whom you can be accountable and let them join you in your desire to grow into Christ's likeness.

NOTES

1. N. T. Wright, *Following Jesus: Biblical Reflections on Discipleship* (Lon-don: SPCK, 1994), 72.

2. These words come from Krister Stendahl, "The Apostle Paul and the Introspective Conscience of the West," in *Paul Among Jews and Gentiles and Other Essays* (Philadelphia: Fortress, 1976) 78–96.

3. See also Ps 51, where David speaks of his "sin as ever before me" (v. 3) and of his having "done what is evil" (v. 4). But he also knows the source of such sin, the evil heart, which he refers to in vv. 5–6.

4. See the discussion in *GEP* of Gal 5:13–15, 16–17, 19–23, 24–26; 6:7–10; Rom 7:4–6; 8:4, 5–8; 13:11–14; Phil 3:3.

5. For further reference to recent scholarship on this question, especially the position of J. D. G. Dunn, to which some of the following is a response, see Fee, *GEP*, 816–22.

6. But does so inconsistently. It uses "sinful nature" when "flesh" implies a negative moral judgment (e.g., see 1 Cor 5:5; Gal 5:13, 16, 17 [twice], 19, 24; 6:8; Rom 7:5–8:13; Col 2:11, 13; Eph 2:3), but "worldly point of view" in 2 Cor 5:16 (cf. 1:12, 17; 10:2) and "flesh" in Phil 3:3–4!

7. This contrast does not occur nearly as often as we are sometimes led to believe, being found basically in Gal 5:13–6:10 (cf. the analogy in 4:29); Rom 8:3–17; and Phil 3:3—although see also 1 Cor 3:1.

POWER IN WEAKNESS— THE SPIRIT, PRESENT WEAKNESS, AND PRAYER

Present eschatological existence is lived in the radical middle, in the midst of all kinds of present weaknesses knowing the power of the Spirit, who especially comes to our aid in prayer.

Two true stories. The first took place in the dim past when I was in college. Stan was in his mid-twenties, married, a vital member of our local church, but he lay dying from a large tumor on his spine. I went to visit him with fear and trepidation. I was scarcely twenty, knew little about death and dying, and certainly knew that I was too young to be of much comfort. But I went because he was also my friend, and I am a Pentecostal, who believes that God heals the sick.

I have never forgotten my experience that day, for what happened to me happened to all who visited him. We went with due apprehension, not knowing what to say; but Stan's own experience of Christ's presence, what he was learning about God's love, and his readiness—dare I say a kind of Pauline eagerness—to be with his Lord was so infectious that we all left Stan's presence built up in our God. We went to comfort him; we left having been ministered to by him. He died three months later, a Pentecostal who also trusted to the very end that God might show him mercy through healing; but he died without disillusionment, because he was ready to enter his eternal reward.

The second story happened many years later, when our oldest son was in college, and home for the holidays. It was a Sunday morning, and he had decided to "have church" in front of the TV, located in the basement family room. He let out a whoop, which caused Maudine and me to rush pell-mell downstairs. There on the screen was the wife of one of the then well-known televangelists. When we got there, she was pointing her finger at the television audience with a brittle harshness. "If any of you out there are dying of cancer," she nearly shouted, "it's your fault, not God's. God wants to heal you."

Two stories; two followers of Christ. I prefer the first.

At issue in this chapter is the relationship between the Spirit as God's empowering presence and the theme of weakness in Paul. Here in particular it is easy to miss the radical middle in which Paul himself walked and to err with un-Pauline emphases on one side or the other. My point, one will not be surprised to read by now, is that our present eschatological existence—our experience of God's kingdom "already but not yet realized" in the life of the church—is also the key to this final set of contrasts in Paul. Again, the presence of the eschatological Spirit plays a major role, although in this case also resulting in some tensions for later believers.

THE PRESENT SITUATION

There are two more or less clearly defined sides on the issue of the Spirit and present weakness. On the one hand stands a view that by default is easily that of the majority.[1] This view has a subtlety to it that makes it look more Pauline than it actually is; indeed, it leans toward a defeatism that is especially difficult to square with Paul. At issue here is a tendency on the part of some to confuse the term "weakness," that is, life *in* the flesh, with life *according to* the flesh. When Paul says, for example, that "the Spirit assists us in our weakness" (Rom 8:26), "weakness" is taken to encompass all of our present existence, including our sinfulness. Paul's glorying in his weaknesses is then seen to embrace the alleged Spirit-flesh struggle as well as the various bodily weaknesses and sufferings to which Paul actually refers.[2]

But Paul never makes that equation, as any careful study of the term "weakness" in Paul demonstrates.[3] This term does indeed apply to life *in* the flesh, that is, our present human life that is still lived in the context of suffering and disability. But as noted in the preceding chapter, life *in* the flesh is not the same as life *according* to the flesh, which in Paul means to live in sin.

The best evidence that Paul does not include an inner Spirit-flesh conflict within his understanding of being empowered in weakness is that he can speak positively of living in weakness, so much so that it is for him a cause for "boasting/glorying" and thus for joy. It is unimaginable that he should rejoice over life according to the flesh—nor in fact does he do so.

That suffering and pain stem from evil is not to be doubted; that they are the direct result of our own evil—or lack of faith, as some would have it—is not only to be doubted but to be vigorously rejected as completely foreign to Paul.

The result of this view is an under-realized eschatological perspective—with so much emphasis on the not yet that there is little on the already. Even though there is much talk about the Spirit on this side, there is a strong tendency to leave God's people to slug it out in the trenches more or less on their own, with some lip service paid to the Spirit but with little of Paul's experience of the Spirit as the empowering presence of God.

On the other side lie some equally strong tendencies toward triumphalism—an exaggerated, sometimes exclusive, focus on the already. This extreme is a special temptation in a culture like late-twentieth-century North America, which rejects pain of any kind as a form of evil and avoids suffering at all costs. Here the difficulty is not between an internal struggle and a human tendency to sinfulness, but between the promised—and experienced—power of the Holy Spirit and our culture's view of suffering and pain as inherently evil.

That suffering and pain stem from evil is not to be doubted; that they are the direct result of our own evil—or lack of faith, as some would have it—is not only to be doubted but to be vigorously rejected as completely foreign to Paul. The result of this view is something of an over-realized eschatological perspective, emphasizing the already to the neglect of the not yet, resulting in an un-Pauline view of the Spirit as present in power while negating weakness in the present as dishonoring to God.

The problem here lies with the tendency to separate some realities that in Paul gladly coexist.[4] Paul knows nothing of a gospel that is not at the same time God's power, power manifested through the resurrection of Christ and now evidenced through the presence of the Spirit. That includes "miracles" in the assembly (Gal 3:5), to which Paul can appeal in a matter-of-fact way as proof that salvation in Christ is based on faith, not on Torah observance ("He who supplies you with the Spirit and performs miracles among you, is it on the basis of works of law or of the hearing of faith?"). It also includes the effective proclamation of Christ accompanied by the Spirit's manifest power in bringing about conversions (1 Thess 1:5-6; 1 Cor 2:4-5), despite the obvious weakness of the messenger himself (1 Cor 2:1-3; 2 Cor 12:7-10).

For many, especially the Corinthians (and their legion of present-day followers), the latter seems a contradiction in terms. How can there be miracles, but no miracle in one's own behalf? How can one glory in the power of the resurrection and the life of the Spirit and not have that power applied to one's own physical weaknesses and suffering? "Physician, heal thyself" was not just a word spoken to Christ. It is always the bottom line of those for whom God's power can be manifest only in visible and extraordinary ways, who never consider that God's greater glory rests on the manifestation of his grace and power through the weakness of the human vessel, precisely so that there will never be any confusion as to the source!

THE SPIRIT, POWER, AND WEAKNESS

We begin by looking at the word "power," since part of our problem is again one of definitions. We cannot always be sure what power might have meant for Paul. It refers frequently to visible manifestations that reveal the Spirit's presence (e.g., 1 Cor 2:4–5; Gal 3:5; Rom 15:19). The evidence from 1 Thessalonians 5:19–22; 1 Corinthians 12–14; Galatians 3:2–5; and Romans 12:6 makes certain that the Pauline churches were "charismatic" in the sense that a dynamic presence of the Spirit was manifested in their gatherings.[5] Even where power means that believers grasp and live out the love of Christ in a greater way (Eph 3:16–20), Paul recognizes here a miraculous work of the Spirit whose evidence will be the way renewed people behave toward one another. This dynamic, evidential dimension of life in the Spirit probably more than anything else separates believers in later church history from those in Paul's churches. Whatever else, the Spirit was *experienced* in Paul's churches; he was not simply part of a phrase in the creed.

The Spirit was experienced in Paul's churches; he was not simply part of a phrase in the creed.

Nevertheless, Paul also assumes the closest link between the Spirit's power and present weaknesses. Without explicitly saying so, passages such as Romans 8:17–27 and 2 Corinthians 12:9 indicate that the Spirit is seen as the source of empowering in the midst of affliction or weakness. In Paul's view, knowing Christ means both knowing the power of his resurrection and participating in his sufferings (Phil 3:9–10); indeed, one needs to know the former to embrace the latter. God's concern for us in the present is that we live cruciform, "conformed to Christ's likeness in his death" (Phil 3:10), as that has been illustrated in the glorious story of Christ in 2:6–11. Suffering means to be as the Lord, following his example and thus "filling up what was lacking in his sufferings" (Col 1:24).

Nonetheless, Paul also expects God's more visible demonstration of power, through the Spirit, to be manifested even in the midst of weakness, as God's proof that his power resides in the message of a crucified Messiah. In 1 Corinthians 2:3-5, therefore, Paul can appeal simultaneously to the reality of his own weaknesses and the Spirit's manifest power in his preaching and in the Corinthians' conversion; and in 1 Thessalonians 1:5-6, he reminds these new believers that they became so by the power of the Spirit, but in the midst of suffering that was also accompanied by the joy of the Holy Spirit.

All of this reflects Paul's basic eschatological understanding of Christian existence as already/not yet, a tension that Paul was able to keep together in ways that many later Christians can not. For him it was not simply tension in which the present was all weakness and the (near) future all glory. The future had truly broken into the present, as verified by the gift of the Spirit; and since the Spirit meant the presence of God's power, that dimension of the future had already arrived in some measure. Thus present suffering is a mark of discipleship, whose model is our crucified Lord. But the same power that raised the Crucified One from the dead is also already at work in our mortal bodies.

This paradox in Paul's understanding is what creates so many difficulties for moderns. We have tended to emphasize one to the neglect of the other. Paul, and the rest of the New Testament writers, hold these expressions of Spirit and power in happy tension. After all, for Paul, the preaching of the Crucified One is the working center of God's power in the world (1 Cor 1:18-25), and Paul's own preaching in a context of weakness and fear and trembling certified that the power which brought about the Corinthians' conversion lay in the work of the Spirit, not in the wisdom or eloquence of the preacher. Paul thus steers a path through the radical middle that is often missed by both Evangelicals and Pentecostals, who traditionally misplace their emphasis on one side or the other.

Whether or not a (sometime) companion of Paul, the author of the epistle to the Hebrews seems to capture this paradox in a slightly different way, through the several examples of faith (= faithfulness, perseverance) in 11:32-38. Some lived "in faith" and saw great miracles performed; others also lived "in faith" and were tortured and put to death. But all were commended for their faith, the author concludes. So with the Spirit and power in Paul. The Spirit means the presence of great power, power to overflow with hope (Rom 15:13), power sometimes attested by signs and wonders and at other times by joy in great affliction. However, precisely because the Spirit has not brought the final End, but only the beginning of the End, power does not mean final perfection in the present age; rather it leads to maturity in Christ.

The Spirit means the presence of great power, power to overflow with hope (Rom 15:13), power sometimes attested by signs and wonders and at other times by joy in great affliction.

Thus the whole of Paul's understanding of our present life in the Spirit, paradoxical as it may seem at times, is put into proper perspective if we begin, as we should, with chapters 2 and 5 above—by realizing that the Spirit is both the fulfillment of the eschatological promises of God and the down payment on our certain future. We are both already and not yet. The Spirit is the evidence of the one, the guarantee of the other.

To our great delight we are not left to ourselves, looking for ways merely to cope as we live in the radical middle. Nor is the Spirit present simply to give us a show of power now and then as a reminder that we belong to the future after all. Rather he is present as our constant companion, both to lead and to empower us. At no point is this empowering more significant than in our life of prayer.

THE SPIRIT AND PRAYER[6]

Throughout this book I have tried to point out that the division often perceived in the church between the corporate people of God and the individual is a false one as far as Paul's experience and theology are concerned. Those who emphasize more the corporate side of things also sometimes shy away from, or are uncomfortable with, personal piety, including "Spirituality." All pietistic movements (historical movements strongly concerned with individual spirituality) come into being in reaction to a tendency for the individual's relationship with God to get lost or swallowed up in some form of churchiness. Nowhere is this more obvious than in the attitude of some toward prayer.

One of the more remarkable inconsistencies in studies on Paul is that thousands of books exist that search every aspect of Paul's thinking, while only a few seek to come to terms with his life of prayer. Indeed, most people's understanding of Paul is limited either to Paul the missionary or to Paul the theologian. But what is clear from Paul's letters is that he was a *pray-er* before he was a missioner or a thinker. His life was devoted to prayer; and his relationship with his converts was primarily sustained by way of thanksgiving and prayer. To eliminate prayer from Paul's personal piety would be to investigate the workings of a gas-combustion engine without recognizing the significance of oil. Paul did not simply believe in prayer or talk about prayer. He prayed, regularly and continuously, and urged the same on his churches (1 Thess 5:16–18). Although this is undoubtedly a carryover from his life before Christ, what we need to note here is that for Paul prayer has been radically transformed by the coming of the Spirit.

> *What is clear from Paul's letters is that he was a* pray-er *before he was a missioner or a thinker.*

Whether set prayers were ever said in Paul's churches cannot be known; in any case, spontaneous prayer by the Spirit is the norm.[7] The beginning of Christian life is marked by the indwelling Spirit's crying out "*Abba*" to God (Gal 4:6; Rom 8:15). "On all occasions," Paul urges elsewhere, "pray in/by the Spirit"; this injunction applies to every form of prayer (Eph 6:18), including prayer for the enabling of evangelism.

With prayer in particular the Spirit helps us in our already/not yet existence. Because in our present weakness we do not know how or for what to pray, the Spirit himself makes intercession for us with "inarticulate groanings" (Rom 8:26–27), an expression that most likely refers to glossolalia (speaking in tongues).

Prayer (and praise), therefore, seems the best way to view Paul's understanding of glossolalia. At no point in 1 Corinthians 14 does Paul suggest that tongues is speech directed toward people;[8] three times he indicates that it is speech directed toward God (14:2, 14–16, 28). In vv. 14–16 he specifically refers to tongues as "praying with my S/spirit"; and in v. 2 such prayer is described as "speaking mysteries to God," which is why the *mind* of the speaker is left unfruitful, and also why such prayer without interpretation is not to be part of the corporate setting. Paul himself engaged in such prayer so frequently that he can say boldly to a congregation who treasured this gift that he prayed in tongues more than any of them (1 Cor 14:18). To be sure, he will also, he insists, "pray with my mind." What he will *not* do is engage in only one form of prayer, as most later Christians have tended to do.

Further, prayer in the Spirit does not mean to be in "ecstasy";[9] it means the Spirit's praying through his spirit without the burden of his mind and in conversation with God. We can trust the Spirit in such prayer, he argues in Romans 8:26–27, precisely because such prayer is a form of the Spirit's assisting us in our weaknesses, and God knows the mind of the Spirit, that he prays in keeping with God's will.

Praying "in the Spirit" (however that is understood) is also God's provision for his people in another area of weakness—in the ongoing struggle "against the principalities and powers." Besides the defensive armor provided by the gospel, Paul urges the believers to use their two "Spirit weapons" as they engage the enemy: the message of the gospel (penetrating the enemy's territory and rescuing people who are captive to him) and "praying in the Spirit" (Eph 6:18–20).

Here in particular the Spirit is our true friend and aid. Precisely because we do not know how to pray as we ought, we need to lean more heavily on praying in/by the Spirit to carry on such spiritual warfare more effectively. Prayer, therefore, is not simply our cry of desperation or our grocery list of requests that we bring before our heavenly *Abba;* prayer is an activity inspired by God himself, through his Holy Spirit. It is God siding with his people and, by his own empowering presence, the Spirit of God himself, bringing forth prayer that is in keeping with his will and his ways.

It is probably impossible to understand Paul as a theologian, if one does not take this dimension of his "Spirit-uality" with full seriousness. A prayerless life is one of practical atheism. As one who lived in and by the Spirit, Paul understood prayer in particular to be the special prompting of the Spirit, leading him to thanksgiving for others and petition in the Spirit, even when he did not know for what specifically to pray. Whatever else life in the Spirit meant for Paul, it meant a life devoted to prayer, accompanied by joy and thanksgiving.

Prayer, after all, is the ultimate expression of our life between the times. It is evidence of our utterly dependent status; as it is also evidence of our continuing in the present in recognized weakness. Prayer in the Spirit does not make demands upon God (though our prayers often do), but humbly waits and listens to God—and trusts God the Holy Spirit to intercede for us in keeping with God's own will and pleasure.

A prayerless life is one of practical atheism.

In this context we should perhaps also include one of the dimensions of Paul's Spirituality that is most difficult to evaluate, the place of visions and revelations. We know about these only because Paul is stepping over onto the Corinthians' turf momentarily in order to persuade them that it is totally inappropriate to use such experiences to authenticate his—or anyone else's—apostleship (2 Cor 12:1–10).[10] What we need to note is that Paul clearly affirms that he has had such experiences and apparently has had them often; but he disallows that they have any value at all in authenticating ministry.

Much as with glossolalia, therefore, we learn about such matters in his life in the Spirit only because the Corinthians made too much of them. Obviously for Paul both of these kinds of Spirit experiences belonged to his private relationship with God; thus he simply never speaks about them on his own. "Ecstasy" for him was a matter between himself and God; before others he will only be "sober-minded" (2 Cor 5:13).

How different from so much of church history! A parade of private Spirit experiences has all too often been the first credential brought forward to authenticate ministry or spirituality. Paul could point to plenty of Spirit activity that had to do with God's dealings with others, usually from within a context of personal weakness. Thus such moments as those described in the modest terms of 2 Corinthians 12:1-6 were undoubtedly moments highlighting the richness of his life in the Spirit, life for him in the personal presence of God. But these were too private to be either promoted or paraded. That he "knew such a man" who had been "transported to the third heaven" must have been a regular source of personal encouragement. But he also knew how to keep quiet about it, because being conformed to Christ's death through the power of the resurrection is what life in the present is all about.

—

At the end we need to note again, however, that even Paul's own life of prayer in the Spirit is known to us because the Corinthians were blowing it in their corporate life. That is what he speaks to in 1 Corinthians 14; we learn of his private practice coincidentally as he addresses what for him was the larger issue. That brings us to the final matters regarding the Spirit in Paul—the gathered church as a place where the Spirit is manifestly present, leading the church to praise God and edify one another.

NOTES

1. The default, it seems to me, stems from a general failure to take the Spirit seriously as God's empowering presence.

2. The chief proponent of this view is J. D. G. Dunn, *Jesus and the Spirit* (Philadelphia: Westminster, 1975) 326-42, who for all his powerful moments and keen insights nonetheless makes a confusion at this point that is simply foreign to Paul.

3. In this regard see D. A. Black, *Paul, Apostle of Weakness: Astheneia and Its Cognates in the Pauline Literature* (American University Studies; New York: Peter Lang, 1984).

4. I say "gladly" not because Paul enjoyed suffering, but because he saw suffering distinctly in terms of discipleship. That is, he saw suffering as following in the ways of Christ, who suffered before entering into his

glory, and who through that suffering redeemed the people of God. Hence Paul's willingness not only to suffer for Christ's, and thus the church's, sake, but to rejoice in suffering, inasmuch as it confirmed for him the reality of his discipleship.

5. On this matter see chs. 13 and 14 below; cf. Dunn, *Jesus*, 160–65.

6. On this question see Fee, "Some Reflections on Pauline Spirituality," in *Alive to God: Studies in Spirituality Presented to James Houston* (ed. J. I. Packer and L. Wilkinson; Downers Grove, Ill.: InterVarsity, 1992) 96–107. See also K. Stendahl, "Paul at Prayer," in *Meanings: The Bible as Document and as Guide* (Philadelphia: Fortress, 1984) 151–61; and more recently, D. A. Carson, *A Call to Spiritual Reformation: Priorities from Paul and His Prayers* (Grand Rapids: Baker, 1992).

7. It has sometimes been noted, as a word either against the personality of the Spirit or against Paul's trinitarianism, that the Spirit is never invoked in prayer, as are the Father and the Son. Precisely, but the conclusion being drawn is incorrect. The role of the Spirit in prayer is a different one; he is our divine "pray-er," the one *through* whom we pray, not the one *to* whom prayer is directed.

8. See further the exegesis of 1 Cor 14:5 in *GEP*, where I argue that the interpretation of a tongue does not thereby turn it into human-directed speech, but interprets the mystery spoken to God referred to in 14:2.

9. This term is used here in its more technical sense of having some sort of transcendent, out-of-body experience of God.

10. See the discussion of 2 Cor 5:13 in *GEP*, 327–30.

TO THE PRAISE OF HIS GLORY—THE SPIRIT AND WORSHIP

*The Spirit gathers the newly constituted people of God
in worship for corporate praise of God and sharing
of gifts to build up the community of faith.*

Growing up in a Pentecostal church was a marvelous, and in-triguing, experience. Because the experiential nature of our faith appealed especially to many who were otherwise marginalized, both in society at large and in the mainline churches, the diversity Paul speaks of in 1 Corinthians 12 was our common lot. With that diversity came many strange things in church, not all of them edifying to the body, and some of them downright scary for some of us. When those of us from my generation raised in this tradition get together, we often swap stories and laugh till we hurt, not a hurtful, mocking laughter, but in joyous remembrance of the idiosyncrasies of some of God's dearest people.

There was "ow-ooo Ferris," a dear brother, who when he got blessed yelled "ow-ooo," while sort of dancing in place and out into the aisle. There was brother Lawrence, whose sudden grasp of the glory of what was being preached (by my father in this case) erupted in a shouted "hallelujah" so sudden and loud it sent shivers up and down the spine. And then there was the brother who stood up to prophesy some crazy thing, and started, typically, "Thus saith the Lord." When his prophecy was weighed and found wanting, it was gently suggested that perhaps it was not the Lord who had spoken after all. He jumped to his feet again. "Thus saith the Lord," he shouted, "that was too me!" Whatever else, Pentecostal services in our younger days were not dull!

But in the midst of all this there was the other reality, the much greater reality of the presence of God in our midst. At this point we got it absolutely right. We knew by instinct, by our reading of Scripture, and by our experience of the Spirit that life in Christ was a life of joy. To be sure, in contrast with the later charismatic movement, the first response to God's presence was often weeping and repentance. God had come among us, and we were filled with awe. But repentance was followed by joy, because we knew that one of the primary reasons for our gathering together was to express our love and praise to God with bursting thanksgiving and joyful singing. We knew also that the reason for the gifts of the Spirit was to aid us in this praise, as well as to build us up as the people of God for life in the world. If not all that we did was biblical, we were biblical at the heart of things.

For Paul the gathered church was first of all a worshipping community; and the key to their worship was the presence of the Holy Spirit.

In this chapter we explore what Paul says about the Spirit and worship, what biblical worship means. Right up front we need to be clear about two matters, one by way of reminder.

First, as I pointed out in the overture, Paul knows nothing of the kind of either/or pattern that has developed in the later church between fruit and gifts, between ethics and Spirit-inspired worship. Indeed, according to Colossians 3:16 and Ephesians 5:19, one of the ways the community heeded the command to keep filled with the Spirit was to teach and admonish one another regarding the message of Christ through psalms, hymns, and Spirit songs. These passages suggest a much closer relationship to ethics and worship than is sometimes noted. In any case, just as with ethics, so with worship: Paul understands the Spirit to play a leading role.

Second, because of the situational nature of Paul's letters, they contain nothing close to a systematic presentation of the worship of the early church. What we learn is in response to problems and is therefore fragmentary. Nonetheless, for Paul the gathered church was first of all a worshipping community; and the key to their worship was the presence of the Holy Spirit. Thus, in Philippians 3:3, in his strong attack against the "mutilators of the flesh" (through circumcision), Paul begins by asserting that "*we* are the circumcision (i.e., 'the people of God'), who serve/worship by the Spirit of God." *Their* worship is a matter of a religious rite performed in the flesh; *ours* is a matter of Spirit.

The Spirit is seen as responsible for worship (see esp. 1 Cor 14:6, 24, 26); moreover, when believers are assembled in this way, Paul understood himself to be present in S/spirit (probably in the reading of the letter as his prophetic voice among them), along with the "power of the Lord Jesus" (1 Cor 5:3–5; Col 2:5). Thus, even though he makes no direct allusion to the presence of the Spirit at the Lord's Table (1 Cor 10:16–17; 11:17–34), we may assume his understanding of the bread as representing Christ's body the church (10:16–17; 11:29), made so by the Spirit, to lead in that direction. Indeed, one would not be far wrong to see the Spirit's presence at the Table as Paul's way of understanding the real presence. The analogy of Israel's having had "Spiritual food" and "Spiritual drink" in 1 Corinthians 10:3–4 at least allows as much.

In any case, the Spirit is specifically noted as responsible for all other expressions of Christian worship. What Paul says explicitly about worship is what we want to look at here.

SPIRIT-LED WORSHIP

Perhaps most noteworthy from the available evidence[1] is the free, spontaneous nature of worship in Paul's churches, apparently orchestrated by the Spirit himself. Worship is expressed in a variety of ways and with the (potential) participation of everyone (1 Cor 14:26). There is no hint of a worship leader, although that must not be ruled out on the basis of silence. But neither is chaos permitted. The God whom they worship is a God of peace (v. 33), whose character is to be reflected in both the manner and the content of their worship. Therefore, disorder is out. Although all may participate (vv. 23, 24, 26, 31), there are some guidelines.

Speakers of inspired utterances must be limited to two or three at a time, and they must be followed by those who interpret and discern. They must respect one another: speakers must make way for others, since the "S/spirit of the prophet is subject to the prophet" (1 Cor 14:32). Thus spontaneity does not mean lack of order; it means "peace" and "decency and orderliness"—also the work of the Spirit.

In the somewhat puzzling correction in 1 Corinthians 11:2–16, Paul refers to both men and women as "praying and prophesying." The inclusion of "prophesying" presupposes for that passage a setting of the church gathered for worship. Moreover, praying and prophesying are almost certainly to be understood not as delimiting terms but as representative, in this case of the two basic kinds of activities that happened in Christian worship.

In terms of participation, both men and women share equally in the praying and prophesying.

Together they represent the two primary focuses of gathered worship: God and the believing community. Thus prayer (and song and tongues, according to 1 Cor 14:2 and 15) is directed toward God; and prophesying represents the many forms of speech—especially Spirit-inspired speech—that are directed toward the people of God to edify them (1 Cor 14:3, 16) or toward outsiders to influence them to conversion (14:24–25).

Several of the *charismata* ("gracious giftings") discussed in chapter 14 below also belong to the context of worship together as a body. This is especially true of those gifts that involve speech directed toward the community, as Paul's words of correction in 1 Corinthians 14 make clear. These gifts include prophecy, teaching, knowledge, and revelation (v. 6), however we finally define some of these in relationship to others.

In terms of participation, both men and women share equally in the praying and prophesying (1 Cor 11:4–5). In the Christian assembly the cry of Moses has been fulfilled: "I wish that all the Lord's people were prophets and that the Lord would put his Spirit on them!" (Num 11:29 NIV). This is in keeping with 1 Corinthians 14:23, where again somewhat in passing Paul says that "all may prophesy."

The problem in 1 Corinthians 11:5–6, therefore, is not that women pray and prophesy in the assembly, but that they are doing so in appearance similar to men, which Paul considers to be an expression of shame. That women are full participants in the worship of Paul's churches, including the more preferred expression of Spirit-inspired speech, prophecy, moves considerably beyond the norm of Paul's Jewish background and seems to be in keeping with the rest of the New Testament evidence, as little as there is. In terms of ministry within the worshipping community, the Holy Spirit apparently inspires women and men alike, since in Christ Jesus such distinctions have no religious value in God's new end-time kingdom (Gal 3:28).

Since we discussed prayer in the preceding chapter and we will look at prophecy in the following one, in this chapter we note the place of singing in Paul's churches. As with prayer, song had become the specialty of the Spirit (1 Cor 14:14–15, 26; Col 3:16; Eph 5:19). Our interest here is primarily in the twin passages in Colossians and Ephesians.

TEACHING WITH SPIRIT-INSPIRED SINGING

Colossians 3:16 appears toward the conclusion of a series of exhortations (vv. 12–17) that indicate what it means for the believers in Colossae to live as those "raised with Christ" (v. 1). In order for us to catch Paul's emphases, I present the text in a more structured form, indicating how the various parts belong to one another:

Let the word of Christ dwell in your midst richly,
> by teaching
> and
> admonishing one another
> in all wisdom
> with psalms,
> hymns [and]
> Spiritual songs
> by singing to God
> from your hearts
> with gratitude.[2]

That this is what Paul was saying is made clear by the twin passage in Ephesians 5:18–19, where the structure is quite certain:

> but be filled with the Spirit, speaking to one another with psalms and hymns and Spiritual songs, singing and hymning with your hearts to the Lord.

Here are passages full of intriguing information about worship in the Pauline churches.

The Opening Exhortations

We begin with some observations about the opening clauses ("let the word of Christ dwell in your midst richly" and "but be filled with the Spirit") that are of considerable importance.

1. Everything about the contexts, and the language of both sentences in particular, indicate that Paul is here reflecting on the Christian community. These are not words for the individual believer, but for believers as the people of God in relationship with one another. In Colossians that is especially clear. Beginning with 3:12, everything has the community in sight, since everything is for, or in light of, "one another." Thus in the immediately preceding exhortation (v. 15), which sets the pattern for the present one, they are to let the peace of Christ rule in their hearts, since it is to this that they have been called together as one body.

Colossians 3:16 views these relationships within the context of the gathered people of God at worship, where they are to teach and admonish one another as one way that the word of Christ will dwell "in them" richly. This means that the prepositional phrase "in/among you," even though it modifies the verb "indwell" and would ordinarily mean "within you," here means "in your midst." The indwelling "word of Christ," therefore, in its two forms of "teaching and admonishing one another" and of "singing to God," has to do with the church at worship.

If the community context in Ephesians is less immediately certain, it is clearly in view, since the whole passage from 4:1 through chapter 6 takes up community life, how they are to "maintain the unity of the Spirit in the bond of peace" (4:3).

2. In the same vein, it is significant to note that the compound participles, "teaching and admonishing," are the same two that Paul used in Colossians 1:28 to describe his own ministry. Here, then, is clear evidence that Paul did not consider ministry to be the special province of either apostles or officeholders. As in the earliest of his letters (1 Thess 5:14), these kinds of activities in the Christian assembly are the responsibility of all.

This is in keeping with the picture that emerges in 1 Corinthians 14:26 as well. Here he admonishes in a presuppositional way that "when you come together, *each one* has a hymn, [etc.] . . . for the strengthening of the church."

3. The primary concern of the exhortation in the Colossians passage is with the "word of Christ." In Paul this expression invariably means "the message of the gospel with its central focus on Christ." This, after all, is what the letter is all about: Christ the embodiment of God, Christ the all-sufficient one, Christ, creator and redeemer. Paul now urges that this "word of Christ," which in part he has already articulated in 1:15–23, "dwell in their midst" in an abundant way.

In so doing, they will reflect precisely what we learned about worship from 1 Corinthians 11:4–5. Part of their activity will be directed toward one another ("teaching and admonishing one another"), and part toward God ("singing to God with your hearts"). Thus the riches of the gospel are to be present among them with great richness. The structure of the sentence as a whole indicates that songs of all kinds are to play a significant role in that richness.

4. The parallel passage in Ephesians makes explicit what we would have guessed in any case, that Paul considers all this activity to be the result of their being filled with the Spirit. Thus, however we are to understand the adjective "Spiritual" in relation to the various expressions of song, Spirit songs are at least one expression of the Spirit's presence, whose fullness will guide and inspire all of the worship in its several expressions.

The Worship Itself

When we turn from these opening clauses to the rest of the sentences, we learn still more about Paul's understanding of Spirit-inspired worship.

1. We need to note, first of all, that where the Spirit of God is, there is also singing. The early church was characterized by its singing; so also in every generation where there is renewal by the Spirit a new hymnody breaks forth. If most such songs do not have staying power, some of them do, and these become the treasure-trove of our on-going teaching and admonishing of

Where the Spirit of God is, there is also singing.

one another, as well as of our constantly turning to God the Father and God the Son and offering praise by inspiration of the Holy Spirit.

2. Nonetheless, it is doubtful whether we are finally able to draw fine lines between the three words used to describe the singing. The "psalms," for example, may well include the Old Testament Psalter, now taken over into the worship of the Christian communities; but one would be bold indeed to limit the word only to the Psalter. This same word is used for the (apparently) more spontaneous singing of 1 Corinthians 14:26, and its corresponding verb is likewise used in 1 Corinthians 14:15 to refer to Spirit-inspired "praise to God." Thus, even though New Testament usage is undoubtedly conditioned by the fact that the hymns of Israel were called "psalms," there is no good reason to understand it as limited to those hymns. What is suggested by this word is a song that is in praise of God.

So also the word "hymn." In the Greek world, this word was used exclusively of songs sung to deities or heroes, and thus would never be used, for example, of the bawdy songs of the bistro. Therefore "hymns" also refer to singing praise to/about God, or in the case of the New Testament to/about Christ as well, as the evidence from Revelation makes especially clear.[3]

In every generation

where there is renewal

by the Spirit a new

hymnody breaks forth.

The word "songs" covers the whole range of singing, so Paul qualifies it here with reference to the Spirit. The adjective *pneumatikos* ("S/spiritual") in Paul ordinarily refers to the Spirit, either directly or indirectly. Here in particular, as most recognize, the ordinary meaning prevails. We are dealing with songs that are inspired by the Spirit. This is most likely an indication of a kind of charismatic hymnody, similar to that alluded to in 1 Corinthians 14:15–16 and 26, in which Spirit-inspired, hence often spontaneous, songs were offered in the context of congregational worship.

Therefore, even though "Spiritual" could well modify all three nouns—the psalms and hymns would also be "of the Spirit"—it is more likely that it is intended to modify "songs" only, referring especially to this one kind of Spirit-inspired singing. This word, after all, is the one that the recipients of the letter would least likely associate with worship, since it covers the whole range of songs in the Greek world, whereas the other two are usually sung to a deity.

3. We probably have fragments of such psalms, hymns, and Spirit songs embedded in our New Testament documents. The book of Revelation, for example, is full of "new songs" sung to God and to the Lamb. That is almost certainly the case with Ephesians 5:14 and 1 Timothy 3:16 as well. But more significantly for this letter, the considered opinion of most New Testament scholars is that Colossians 1:15–18 also reflects such a hymn about Christ.[4] If this is so, and there are no good reasons to doubt it, then that would also explain why Paul thinks of these various kinds of hymns and Spirit songs as a means of their "teaching and admonishing one another." Such songs are at the same time

creedal, full of theological grist, and give evidence of what the early Christians most truly believed about God and his Christ.

4. The background to such two-dimensional worship, hymns that are at once directed toward God and a means of teaching and admonishing one another, is to be found in the Old Testament Psalter. There we find dozens of examples of hymns addressed to God in the second person, which also have sections in the third person, extolling the greatness or faithfulness of God for the sake of those singing to him.[5]

The use of hymns in the New Testament documents indicates how clearly they also function in this two-dimensional way for the early church. Most of them are about Christ, and as such are both in worship of him and for the continuing instruction of God's people. The clear implication of 1 Corinthians 14:15–16 and 26 is that "Spirit songs" in the Pauline communities are also to be understood in this way. Singing "with the mind" (singing intelligible words by the Spirit) is understood as praise to God, and something to which the rest respond with the Amen; and the "psalm" in 14:26 is precisely for the "building up" of the others. Unfortunately, many contemporary Christians do not think of their singing in these terms, and thus miss out on one of the significant dimensions of our reason for singing.

The same Spirit who applied salvation now helps to initiate response through Spirit-inspired songs reflecting the message about Christ, and all to the praise of God.

5. Finally—and with this observation we bring the contents of this book full circle—in its own nonreflective way, Colossians 3:16 too is a trinitarian text. But in contrast to the various texts cited in chapter 4 above, where the Father initiates salvation, which the Son effects and the Spirit applies, here the order is reversed. Christ still plays the central role, hence they must let the "word of Christ" dwell lavishly in their midst. But the same Spirit who applied salvation now helps to initiate response through Spirit-inspired songs reflecting the message about Christ, and all to the praise of God.

The God who created and redeemed is worthy of all praise. The Spirit, who was present at creation and came to bring us to life in redemption, now leads us in the worship and praise of our Redeemer and Creator. In Paul, therefore, our worship is as trinitarian as our experience and our theology. It is obviously the presence of the Spirit among us as we gather in Christ's name that makes it so.

NOTES

1. I stress the factor of available evidence, because what comes to us does so for the most part in the form of correction. We simply do not know enough to make far-reaching, all-inclusive statements about the nature of worship in Paul's churches.

2. For the argumentation in favor of this structure, see *GEP*, 648–57.

3. Even though the word "hymn" itself does not occur. See esp. in this regard Rev 4:11, which is addressed to God and introduced with "saying," and Rev 5:9, which picks up the identical language but is introduced, "they sing a new song, saying . . . " See also 5:12, 13.

4. See most recently N. T. Wright, "Poetry and Theology in Colossians 1.15–20," *New Testament Studies* 36 (1990) 444–68.

5. This happens throughout the Psalter. See, e.g., Ps 30, which offers praise to God in the second person in vv. 1–3, then encourages singing on the part of the congregation in vv. 4–5, predicated on the fact that "his favor lasts a lifetime," and returns to second person address in vv. 6–9. Cf. inter alia Pss 32, 66, 104, 116; so also the many hymns that call on the congregation to praise God in light of his character and wondrous deeds.

THOSE CONTROVERSIAL GIFTS? THE SPIRIT AND THE *CHARISMATA*

Because the Spirit was present with his people,
for Paul his giftings were as normal as breathing
and were intended for the building of the people
in the present as they await the consummation.

One of the fads among evangelicals in the final decades of the twentieth century has been that of finding your spiritual gift. There was hardly a church or youth group that did not have such a conference or seminar. While I appreciate the motivation behind this movement, that each of us recognize and appreciate our role in the church, nonetheless the New Testament scholar in me winced on more than one occasion. I could not imagine Paul understanding what was going on at all!

My problems with this fad are several: taking the texts out of context, rearranging the gifts under our own convenient groupings, thus leveling the various passages in Paul into card-catalogue form, and focusing on discovering what the Corinthians would have known by experience. But the greatest problem for me is the nearly universal tendency to divorce the list of "Spirit manifestations" (Paul's own term in context) in 1 Corinthians 12:8–10 from its clear setting of Christian worship.

We noted in the preceding chapter that community worship includes several extraordinary phenomena, which Paul variously calls *charismata* ("gracious giftings," 1 Cor 12:4),[1] *pneumatika* ("things of the Spirit," 1 Cor 12:1; 14:1), or "manifestations of the Spirit" (1 Cor 12:7). Such phenomena are especially the activity of the Spirit *in the gathered community,* as 1 Corinthians 14 makes abundantly clear.

This is an area, however, where there is also great diversity in understanding, both among scholars and within church contexts. The primary reason for this diversity is the basic assumption by most that Paul is intending to give *instruction* on the meaning and use of *charismata* in the various passages in his letters where this word occurs. What we have in fact is *correction* aimed at particular problems in particular churches; it is not systematic, nor does it cover all bases. Here our concern is to describe the phenomena as best we can in light of the available evidence.

This chapter, therefore, is not intended to cover the whole waterfront. We will focus on the various lists in 1 Corinthians 12–14, although at the outset I will cast the net a bit farther. As with the list of fruit (ch. 10 above), the lists in 1 Corinthians must first of all be understood in their context in 1 Corinthians 12–14, before I offer more general conclusions as to what each of the gifts is about.

HOW MANY GIFTS, AND WHAT KINDS?

Several things need to be said about the various lists in 1 Corinthians 12–14. First, none of them is intended to be complete, as though Paul were setting forth everything that might legitimately be called a "gift of the Spirit." This is proved in part by the fact that no two lists are identical. It goes beyond the evidence—and Paul's own concerns—to speak of "the nine spiritual gifts."

Second, the items in 12:8–10 are called "manifestations of the Spirit," which in context means, "different ways the Spirit shows himself when the community is gathered together." Paul's point here is the community's need for diversity. The list is especially tailored to the situation in Corinth. Paul's grammar and wording suggest a listing in three parts. The first two parts pick up words that held high court in Corinth ("wisdom" and "knowledge") and seem to be an attempt by Paul to recapture these realities for the Spirit and the gospel. The next five have in common that they are, like speaking in tongues (glossolalia), extraordinary phenomena. Finally, after diversity is well heard, he includes the problem child, tongues, along with its necessary companion—at least in the community—the interpretation of tongues.

Third, attempts to categorize the items in the different lists are tentative at best. When those in Romans 12:6–8 and Ephesians 4:11 are included as well, a wide variety of terminology is used (motivational, ministerial, etc.) that the apostle would scarcely recognize and that at best are suspect. The broad spectrum of phenomena are best grouped under the three natural headings hinted at in 1 Corinthians 12:4–6: service, miracles, and inspired utterance. Paul does not refer to visionary experiences such as one finds in 2 Corinthians 12:1–6 as *charismata*, although they belong legitimately to a discussion of Spirit phenomena. Nor does he call people (for example, apostles, pastors) *charismata*; to be sure, they are gifts to the church, as Ephesians 4:11 shows, but only their ministries, not the people themselves, are legitimately termed *charismata*, in Paul's usage.

Forms of Service

Items listed here include "helpful deeds" and "acts of guidance" from 1 Corinthians 12:28; see also "serving," "giving," and "caring for" (in the sense of leadership) in Romans 12:7–8. These are the least visibly "charismatic" of the gifts and the least obvious as expressions of corporate worship. They belong to Paul's ever-present interest in relationships within the church. Thus they are Spirit activity, not so much in the sense of Spirit manifestations within the assembly as in the sense of the broad range of Spirit activity noted in chapters 9 and 10 above. To include them in a discussion of *charismata* would legitimize discussing any and all works of the Spirit as *charismata*, making the category useless.

The Miraculous

Included here are three items from 1 Corinthians 12:9–10, "faith," "gifts of healings," and "workings of miracles." As the recurrence in 13:2 makes certain, "faith" in this list refers to the supernatural gift of faith that can "move mountains." "Gifts of healings" refer to the healing of the physical body (the healing of mind and spirit are for Paul what conversion is about), and "workings of miracles" to all other such phenomena not included in healing.

The use of the plurals, "gifts" and "workings," for the last two probably means that these gifts are not permanent, but each occurrence is a gift in its own right. That such phenomena were a regular part of the apostle's own ministry is demonstrated in 2 Corinthians 12:12 and Romans 15:18–19. That they were also the regular expectation of Paul's churches is demonstrated in Galatians 3:5. He would simply not have understood the presence of the Spirit that did not also include such evidences of the Spirit's working that he termed "powers," which we translate "miracles."

> *Paul would simply not have understood the presence of the Spirit that did not also include such evidences of the Spirit's working that he termed "powers," which we translate "miracles."*

Whether one believes such things happened depends almost entirely on one's worldview. The so-called Enlightenment has had its innings, and moderns, helped along by the phenomenal advances of modern scientific discovery, are prone to unbridled arrogance. That is, Paul and his churches believed in such things, we are told, because of their "primitive" worldview, which moderns casually dismissed as unrealistic. For example, Rudolf Bultmann, speaking for many, caricatured the "three-storeyed universe" of Paul and his contemporaries. This modern worldview is widespread. Many evangelicals, who were incensed at Bultmann's rationalism that so casually dismissed Paul's affirmations of such works of the Spirit, adopted their own brand of rationalism to explain the absence of such phenomena in their own circles: by limiting this kind of Spirit activity to the age of the apostles.

But in defense of Paul, two matters about his affirmations of extraordinary Spirit manifestations must be noted. First, all such statements in Paul are sober, matter-of-fact, and usually off-handed, events that for him would have been open to investigation had anyone felt the need to do so. The reason for this is very simple—and theological. He was born and raised within a (Jewish) tradition that believed in God and could not even have imagined God as not being all-powerful. With this view of God as one who took an active interest in his universe and in the affairs of his people, it would never have occurred to Paul that the one who chose to be present with them in the incarnation and now by his Spirit would do otherwise than graciously step in and work in his people's lives. Those who believe in God as creator and sustainer, but who balk at the miraculous both past and present, have created theological positions for themselves that are difficult to sustain and quite removed from the biblical perspective.

Those who need an occasional miracle to keep their belief in God alive and those who feed on such "faith" by promoting the miraculous as authenticating their "gospel" also lie outside Paul's perspective.

Second, Paul's affirmations about miracles are not the statements of one who is trying to prove anything. That is, he does not point to miracles as grounds for accepting either his gospel or his ministry; on the contrary he rejects such criteria as authenticating ministry of any kind. The cross, with the subsequent resurrection, and the present gift of the Spirit are all the authentication he ever appeals to. Those who need an occasional miracle to keep their belief in God alive and those who feed on such "faith" by promoting the miraculous as authenticating their "gospel" also lie outside Paul's perspective. His view expects and accepts, but does not demand, and on this matter refuses to put God to the test.

Inspired Utterance

Included here are "the message of wisdom," "the message of knowledge," "prophecy," "the discernments of S/spirits," "tongues," and "the interpretation of tongues" from 1 Corinthians 12:8, 10, and "teaching" and "revelation" from 14:6. In light of Ephesians 5:19 and Colossians 3:16, we should probably also include "singing" from 14:26. Attempts to distinguish some of these items from one another are generally futile, as is any distinction between their charismatic or noncharismatic expression (for example, teaching or singing).

The "message of wisdom" and "knowledge" is language created by the situation in Corinth. For Paul the "message of wisdom" refers first of all to the preaching of the cross (see 1 Cor 1:18–2:16; the terminology occurs nowhere else); whether it means some spontaneous expression of Spirit wisdom for the sake of the community is possible, but can never be known. "Knowledge" is closely related to "mysteries" in 1 Corinthians 13:2, and elsewhere it stands close to the concept of "revelation" (13:8–9, 12; 14:6). Similarly, prophecy is closely connected to "revelation" in 14:6 and especially in 14:25, 26, and 30. Are these to be understood as distinctively different gifts? Or, as seems more likely, do they suggest different emphases for the expression of the prophetic gift, since that, too, seems to swing between "revealing mysteries" and more straightforward words of edification, comfort, and exhortation (or encouragement)? In any case, the use of uninterpreted tongues in the assembly is what brought forth the whole argument, and Paul uses prophecy as representative of all other intelligible inspired utterances that are to be preferred to tongues in that setting.

Both because Paul himself uses tongues and prophecy in a running contrast between (edifying) intelligibility and (nonedifying) unintelligibility in 1 Corinthians 14, and because of our inherent interest in these two phenomena, I offer some further suggestions about these two *charismata*.

Speaking in Tongues[2]

Paul's term for this phenomenon is literally "different kinds of tongues." Enough is said in 1 Corinthians 12–14 to give us a fairly good idea as to how he understood it. We have already looked at the role of tongues in Paul's life of prayer (at the end of chapter 12 above). Our interest here is to summarize what he says about it, especially focusing on its role in the community.

1. Whatever else, it is Spirit-inspired utterance; that is made plain by 1 Corinthians 12:7 and 11 and 14:2. This in itself should cause some to speak more cautiously when trying to "put tongues in their place" (usually meaning eliminate them altogether) in the contemporary church. Paul does not damn tongues with faint praise, as some have argued, nor does he stand in awe of the gift, as the Corinthians had apparently done—and some contemporary proponents of tongues do. As with all Spirit-empowered activity, Paul held it in high regard *in its proper place.*

2. The regulations for its community use in 14:27–28 make clear that the speaker is not ecstatic or out of control. Quite the opposite: the speakers must speak in turn, and they must remain silent if there is no one to interpret. Therefore the mind is not detached; but it is at rest and "unfruitful."

3. It is speech essentially unintelligible both to the speaker (14:14) and to other hearers (14:16), which is why it must be interpreted in the assembly.

4. It is speech directed basically toward God (14:2, 14–15, 28); one may assume, therefore, that what is interpreted is not speech directed toward others, but the "mysteries" spoken to God.

5. As a gift for private prayer, Paul held it in the highest regard (14:4, 5, 15, 17–18; cf. Rom 8:26–27; Eph 6:18), as noted in chapter 12 above.

Whether Paul also understood it to be an actual earthly language is a moot point, but the overall evidence suggests not. He certainly does not foresee the likelihood of someone's being present who might understand without interpretation; and the analogy of earthly language in 14:10–12 implies that it is not an earthly language (a thing is not usually identical with that to which it is compared).

Our most likely access to Paul's understanding is through his description of the phenomenon in 1 Corinthians 13:1 as "the tongues of angels." The context virtually demands that this phrase refers to glossolalia or "speaking in tongues." The more difficult matter is its close association with "the tongues of people." Most likely this refers to two kinds of glossolalia: a human dialect, inspired of the Spirit but unknown to the speaker or hearers, and angelic speech, inspired of the Spirit to speak in the heavenly dialect. The historical context in general suggests that the latter is what the Corinthians understood glossolalia to be, and that therefore they considered it one of the evidences of their having already achieved something of their future heavenly status.

Paul shows considerable ambivalence toward this gift. On the one hand, with regard to its use in the public assembly, although he does not condemn it, he is obviously not keen on it. In any case, tongues should not occur at all if there is not an interpretation. On the other hand, as a gift of private prayer and utterance, Paul speaks of tongues quite favorably, obviously a topic that for Paul is very personal and private. The breakdown for him has occurred when what is personal and private comes into the public assembly, since it has no facility for strengthening the others. Here again the central focus on corporate life comes to the fore.

The question as to whether the "speaking in tongues" in contemporary Pentecostal and charismatic communities is the same in kind as that in the Pauline churches is moot—and probably irrelevant. There is simply no way to know. As an *experienced* phenomenon, it is analogous to theirs, meaning that it is understood to be a supernatural activity of the Spirit that functions in many of the same ways, and for its practitioners has value similar to that described by Paul.

Prophecy

Of all the *charismata*, this is the one mentioned most often in Paul's letters. It is specifically mentioned in 1 Thessalonians 5:20; 1 Corinthians 11:4–5; 12:10–14:40; Romans 12:6; Ephesians 2:20; 3:5; 4:11; 1 Timothy 1:18; 4:14; and probably lies behind "through the Spirit" in 2 Thessalonians 2:2 and "in keeping with a revelation" in Galatians 2:2. This implies a wide range of occurrence in Paul's churches.

Although prophecy was also widespread in the Greek world, Paul's understanding is thoroughly shaped by his history in Judaism. The prophet spoke to God's people under the inspiration of the Spirit. In Paul such speech consists of spontaneous, understandable messages, orally delivered in the gathered assembly, intended for the edification or encouragement of the people. For the most part these appear to be directed toward the whole community, although 1 Timothy 1:18 and 4:14 (and probably Gal 2:2) point to words spoken for the sake of individuals—but still within the context of the community.

That the utterances are spontaneous is certain from the evidence in 1 Corinthians 14:29–32, since a "revelation" comes to another while one person is still "prophesying." Those who prophesy are clearly understood to be "in control" (see 14:29–33). Although some people are called "prophets," the implication of 1 Corinthians 14:24–25 and 30–31 is that the gift is available—at least potentially—to all.

But it is also clear that it does not have independent authority. The combined evidence of 1 Thessalonians 5:21–22 and 1 Corinthians 12:10 and 14:29 indicates that all prophesying must be "discerned" by the Spirit-filled community. That is almost certainly the first intent of the gift of the "discernments of S/spirits" in 1 Corinthians 12:10, since the verb form of the noun "discernments" appears in 14:29 as the needed response to prophetic utterances, just as interpretation is needed with tongues.

The actual function of prophecy in the Pauline churches is more difficult to pin down. If our view of Galatians 2:2, 1 Timothy 1:18, and 4:14 is correct, then, on the one hand, the Spirit directs the lives of his servants in specific ways; sometimes they are singled out for the ministry the Spirit empowers (1 Tim 1:18; 4:14), and sometimes they are directed to undertake a difficult mission to Jerusalem (Gal 2:2). On the other hand, the Spirit also reminds the church, probably repeatedly, that the words of Jesus concerning the increase of evil in the end (1 Tim 4:1) are being confirmed. A misguided but heeded prophetic utterance that the day of the Lord had already come (2 Thess 2:2) probably led to the distress in Thessalonica.

In 1 Corinthians 14 yet another picture emerges of how the community regularly experiences the prophetic Spirit: In the case of believers the Spirit speaks encouragement and edification, and in the case of unbelievers he lays bare their hearts in such a way as to lead to repentance. All this textual evidence suggests that prophecy was a widely expressed and widely experienced phenomenon, which had as its goal the building up of the people of God so as to come to maturity in Christ (Eph 4:11–16).[3]

Some recent writing on this issue has been interested in the question of backgrounds and authority. This problem is related to the inspiration and biblical authority of the Old Testament prophets and a concern whether New Testament prophecy should be understood in the same way. Since Paul saw prophecy as evidence for the fulfillment of God's eschatological promises, he undoubtedly also saw the New Testament prophets as in the succession of the legitimate prophets of the Old Testament. This explains in part why all such prophecy must be discerned, just as with those in the Old Testament. But the *nature* of the new prophecy was also understood to be of a different kind, precisely because of the church's present eschatological existence. A prophet who speaks encouragement to the church in its between-the-times existence speaks a different word from the predominant word of judgment on ancient Israel.

The Discernment of Prophecy

In 1 Thessalonians 5:19–22, Paul exhorts: "Do not quench the Spirit; do not despise prophesyings; but test all things, and hold fast to the good and abstain from every evil expression." If the tendency in one sector of the contemporary church is to disobey this injunction by quenching the Spirit through their rejection of prophecy, the tendency on the Pentecostal/charismatic side has been to disregard the rest of the injunctions—which are the main point!

Because of their sense of awe over God's speaking in this way, spontaneously and often in an authoritative kind of voice, Pentecostals have traditionally let almost anything go among them in the name of the Lord. When discernment does happen, it is usually to weed out the bad. Paul's concern lies on both sides, that they discern what the Lord is saying to them so as to hold fast the good, as well as to be done with the bad.

What lies behind this disobedience on the part of the latter traditions is probably a lack of certainty as to the criteria for discernment, as well as a lack of clarity as to how it is to be done. Paul's own criteria emerge in two passages, 2 Thessalonians 2:15 in light of 2:2 and 1 Corinthians 14:3. This latter passage is more easily recognized: those who prophesy do so for the "encouragement (or exhortation), comfort, and edification" of the gathered people of God. A bit more needs to be said about the 2 Thessalonians passages.[4]

The exhortations in 1 Thessalonians are probably given in anticipation of the problem that is spoken to in 2 Thessalonians 2. Although Paul is not sure of the source (prophetic word, his own former teaching, or his earlier letter), someone in the community has gone off half-cocked, and in Paul's name has prophesied that "the day of the Lord has already come." Paul's response to this is 2 Thessalonians 2:3–12, where he reminds them how contradictory that utterance is to his actual teaching while among them. In a summarizing exhortation in v. 15, he then urges them to hold fast to his former teachings, whether they came when he was present among them or from his previous letter. Noticeably absent from this passage is the mention of "Spirit" from v. 2. Paul's point seems clear: they are to weigh all such "Spirit" utterances in light of his own apostolic teaching. I would assume that the same holds true for all believers in all generations.

The worship of the early church was far more "charismatic" than has been true for most of its subsequent history.

How Common Were the Gifts in Paul's Churches?

That Paul can list all these items in such a matter-of-fact way, especially in 1 Corinthians 12:7–11, indicates that the worship of the early church was far more charismatic than has been true for most of its subsequent history. Some indeed have tried to make a virtue of this lack, arguing that the more extraordinary phenomena were relatively limited in the early church—they belong to more "immature" believers like the Corinthians—but are not needed in our more "mature" congregations! But this argument not only misunderstands the childhood/adulthood imagery in 1 Corinthians 13:10–12, it is also by the very nature of Paul's letters a totally invalid argument from silence. One may as well argue that the other churches known to Paul did not celebrate the Lord's Supper, since it is mentioned only in 1 Corinthians (10:16–17; 11:17–34), and as with tongues in 1 Corinthians 12–14 only to correct an abuse.

The evidence is considerable that a visible, charismatic dimension of life in the Spirit was the normal experience of Paul's churches. That Paul should speak to it in a direct way so few times (esp. 1 Thess 5:19–22; 1 Cor 12–14) is an accident of history: they were spoken to only where problems of abuse had arisen. The nature of the problem in Thessalonica, to be sure, is uncertain; either some of them are playing down the prophetic Spirit in their gatherings, or Paul is anticipating some problems and tries to bring it under the rule of "test all things." More likely it is the latter. If so, then it is similar to the problem in Corinth. In any case, Paul's response is never to eliminate such phenomena—they are the manifestations of the Spirit, after all—but to correct by urging proper use.

Even more telling are the offhanded, matter-of-fact ways these phenomena are mentioned elsewhere. For example, in 2 Thessalonians 2:2 Paul knows that someone has falsely informed them as to "the day of the Lord." What he does not know is the source of this false information; one possibility is "through the Spirit" (most likely a nondiscerned prophetic utterance). Likewise in 1 Corinthians 11:2–16 in the matter of head coverings, Paul refers to worship as "praying *and prophesying*," the two primary ways of addressing God and people in the assembly. In Galatians 3:4 he can appeal to their "having experienced so many such things," referring specifically to the experiential dimension of their coming to faith in Christ; and in v. 5 a major point of his argument rests on their ongoing experience of "miracles." Finally, in the case of Timothy's ministry (1 Tim 1:18; 4:14), Timothy's own gifting is related to prophetic utterances in the community. In none of these instances is Paul arguing *for* the gifts; rather, the visible, charismatic expression of their common life in the Spirit is the presupposition *from* which he argues for another point.

We may conclude, therefore, that all the evidence points in one direction: for Paul and his churches the Spirit is the key to their understanding of Christian life, from beginning to end, but above all else the Spirit is experienced, and experienced in ways that are essentially powerful and visible. Although in some cases these Spirit experiences led to triumphalism—of a dualistic type (Spirit against earthly existence)—for Paul these experiences are part of the package. Paul does not ethicize the Spirit, as some have argued;[5] for Paul ethical life by the Spirit is part and parcel of his understanding of the Spirit as the fulfilled eschatological promise of God. That is, the ethical life of the Spirit belonged to the promise and was experienced as such before Paul came to it. His concern is with correction, to ensure that his churches follow in the paths he has taught them from the beginning.

But triumphalism (a belief in assured, constant success and victory in every area of life) was not the necessary result of life in the Spirit, experienced in dynamic and powerfully visible ways, as Paul's own life attests. Here is one who could keep the two together. He could experience the Spirit, visibly manifest among them often and regularly in giftings and empowerings of an extraordinary kind. But at the same time, his continuing fullness of the joy of the Spirit was in the midst of suffering and weaknesses of all kinds.

The Gifts of the Spirit Between the Times

Finally, we need to look at a question that comes from our time, rather than from Paul. Many of the *charismata*, especially the more extraordinary ones (prophecy, healings, miracles, tongues), fell into a time of disuse soon after the apostolic period, only to appear spasmodically thereafter in what many refer to as splinter groups. In our century some have made a virtue of this history, arguing that these gifts belonged to the apostolic period to establish and verify the gospel, but are not needed after the end of the first Christian century, when all the New Testament documents had finally been written.

Interestingly, Paul does speak to this question, in 1 Corinthians 13:8–10, but in a manner unrelated to the way it has been raised in our time. It is not surprising that his answer is once again related to his end-time framework and presuppositions. His solution in this case seems directed against the misguided understanding of *charismata*, especially tongues, on the part of the Corinthians.

In this passage Paul is arguing against the Corinthians' overspiritualized view of the end times. They have apparently emphasized the already in such a way as to negate rather thoroughly the not yet. Already they are rich, full, and have begun to reign (1 Cor 4:8). Tongues seem to serve for them as the "sign" (cf. 14:20–22) of their arrival. For them, speaking the language of angels (13:1) means that they are already partakers of the ultimate state of spiritual existence, leading them to deny a future bodily resurrection (15:12).

As part of his argument against this wrong emphasis on tongues, Paul insists that the gifts do not belong to the (final) future, but only to the present. On this matter the Corinthians are deluded. The irony is that the gifts, to them the evidence of future existence, will pass away when the true future existence is attained (13:8a): the *charismata* are "partial" (v. 9); they are like childhood in comparison with adulthood (v. 11); they are like looking into a mirror in comparison with seeing someone face-to-face (v. 12). But this is not a devaluation of the gifts; rather, it puts them into proper (already but not yet) eschatological perspective. We are still in the present, so in 1 Corinthians 14 Paul not only corrects abuse but also urges proper use. In the present we should pursue love (14:1), because that alone is both for now and forever (13:13); but that also means that in the already we should eagerly desire the Spirit to manifest himself among us by giftings to build up the community. The final glory (what is complete) awaits.

What does not seem possible to extract from this passage is that Paul expected the *charismata* to cease within his lifetime, or shortly thereafter. This particular answer to the issue is raised today not on the basis of reading Scripture, but from the greater concern as to their present legitimacy. But this is a question of worldview, pure and simple, and one that Paul could not have understood. His answer is plain: "Of course they will continue as long as we await the final consummation." Any answer that does not follow in the footsteps of the apostle at this point may hardly appeal to him for support.[6]

———

Paul's word to the Philippians is worth our hearing and heeding today: "Join with others in following my example, brothers and sisters, and take note of those who live according to the pattern we gave you" (3:17). In the context of Philippians that pattern included both "the power of Christ's resurrection and the fellowship of his sufferings" (v. 10). As noted in chapter 10 above, his example of a Spirit-empowered, Spirit-directed life was particularly wide-ranging and included personal Spirituality as well as the community phenomena noted in this chapter. We are already but not yet, and the only way we can so live is by the power of the Spirit. The reason for the gifts in the assembly is to build us up as we live out the life of the future in the present age. The Holy Spirit, as the renewed presence of God, is with us in our gatherings for this very purpose. Thus our final word is like the first one: the Spirit for Paul was an experienced end-time reality who served both as evidence that the future is already at hand and as the guarantee of its final consummation.

> *The reason for the gifts in the assembly is to build us up as we live out the life of the future in the present age.*

NOTES

1. This word does not mean what it is most commonly translated to mean, "gifts of the Spirit." The word has nothing to do with the Spirit on its own; it is a noun formed from the word "grace" and means literally "a concrete expression of grace." It becomes "Spiritual gift" in Rom 1:11 by the addition of the adjective "Spiritual." It is the context of 1 Corinthians, plus the fact that this word is associated with the ministries of the Spirit in 1 Cor 12:4, that has led us to call all these Spirit manifestations in 1 Cor 12 "Spiritual gifts"—properly so in this case, but improperly so in most other occurrences in the New Testament.

2. For bibliography, see *GEP*, 172, n. 336.

3. On the probability that Paul understood himself to be a prophet as well as an apostle, see *GEP* on 1 Cor 14:37 and Eph 3:5. According to 1 Cor 5:3–4 and Col 2:5 he also understood himself to be present by the Spirit in the gathered assembly, presumably at the reading of his letter. Therefore, he probably understood his letters to function in a prophetic way within the churches as they were being read.

4. For the more detailed analysis of these texts see *GEP*, 71–75, or the full argument in my essay "Pneuma and Eschatology in 2 Thessalonians 2.1–2: A Proposal about 'Testing the Prophets' and the Purpose of 2 Thessalonians," in *To Tell the Mystery: Essays on New Testament Eschatology in Honor of Robert H. Gundry* (ed. T. E. Schmidt and M. Silva; *Journal for the Study of the New Testament, Supplement Series* 100; Sheffield: JSOT Press, 1994) 196–215.

5. Especially H. Gunkel, *The Influence of the Holy Spirit*; Ger. original 1888 (ET; Philadelphia: Fortress, 1979). Nor did he, as R. B. Hoyle suggests (*The Holy Spirit in St. Paul* [London: Hodder and Stoughton, 1928] 34), "base all the religious and ethical life of Christians on the quieter, constant, inward working of the Spirit." Paul would not recognize such false distinctions.

6. The most textually perceptive of these various attempts is that by R. Gaffin, *Perspectives on Pentecost* (Philadelphia: Presbyterian and Reformed, 1979). This book basically raises and answers questions, using Paul in support, to which Paul does not speak at all. Compare my critique in *Gospel and Spirit: Issues in New Testament Hermeneutics* (Peabody, Mass.: Hendrickson, 1991) 75–77.

WHERE TO FROM HERE?—THE SPIRIT FOR TODAY AND TOMORROW

*If we are going to count for much in the
post–modern world in which we now live, the
Spirit must remain the key to the church's existence.*

In light of the preceding pages, we must candidly admit that the experience and life of the Spirit were more radically central for Paul and his churches than seems to be true for most of us. The Spirit was more genuinely experienced as well. That awareness has led to the title of this final chapter. Proper humility will also acknowledge that the most appropriate answer to the question is "I don't know."

Rather than try to give answers, therefore, I propose to end (1) by identifying the central features of Paul's approach to the Spirit, (2) by pointing out the frequent distance between Paul and ourselves on these matters, and (3) by offering some brief suggestions about bridging that distance. What is said here assumes the truth of the Reformation principle: the church must be both "reformed and always being reformed." Historically, the most important ingredient of true reformation and renewal is for the church to become more intentionally biblical in its thought and actions.

PAUL'S UNDERSTANDING OF THE SPIRIT: A SUMMARY

The following are what I see to be at the heart of Paul's approach to the Spirit, given now in slightly different order from the way they appear in the preceding chapters:

1. *The Key to Christian Experience.* The most obvious point has been repeated in a number of ways throughout, namely, the crucial role the Spirit plays in Paul's Christian experience and therefore in his understanding of the gospel. In the final analysis, in every aspect of his theology—at least what is basic to his theology—the Spirit plays a leading role. To be sure, the Spirit is not *the* center for Paul—Christ is, ever and always—but the Spirit stands close to the center, making Christ known and empowering all genuinely Christian life and experience. For this reason, the Spirit must play a much more vital role in our thinking about Paul's theology than tends now to be the case.

> In every aspect of Paul's theology—at least what is basic to his theology—the Spirit plays a leading role.

2. *God Breaking into Our Lives.* Equally crucial to Paul's perspective is the *dynamic, experiential* way the Spirit comes into the life of the individual and into the ongoing life of the believing community. This reality lies behind everything Paul says; it is a point Paul presupposes and thus argues from, not for. The Spirit as an experienced reality lies behind both the Corinthian abuse and Paul's correction of Spirit life in that community (1 Cor 12–14); it is basic to his reminding the Thessalonians about the reality of their conversion (1 Thess 1:4–6); it serves as primary evidence that life in Christ is based on faith and apart from Torah (Gal 3:1–5; 4:6–7); it is the assumption lying behind the commands in 1 Thessalonians 5:19–22 (cf. 2 Thess 2:2); it serves as evidence confirming Paul's own ministry as an apostle (1 Cor 2:4–5; 2 Cor 12:12; Rom 15:18–19); it is the basic truth on which Paul can argue for

the sufficiency of life in the Spirit (Gal 5:13–6:10); and it is essential to his reminder to Timothy to fan Spirit life into flame in order to receive the necessary power and courage for ministry in Ephesus (1 Tim 1:18; 4:14; 2 Tim 1:6–7). Both Paul's direct and passing references to the work of the Spirit everywhere presuppose the Spirit as an empowering, experienced reality in the life of the church and the believer.

3. *End-Time Evidence and Guarantee of Glory.* Pivotal to the Spirit's central role is the thoroughly eschatological framework within which Paul both experienced and understood the Spirit. The Spirit had played a leading role in his— and others'—expectations about the end times. Along with the resurrection of Christ, therefore, the outpoured Spirit radically altered Paul's eschatological perspective. On the one hand, the coming of the Spirit fulfilled the Old Testament promises, and was the sure *evidence* that the future had *already* been set in motion; on the other hand, since the final consummation of God's kingdom had *not yet* taken place, the Spirit also served as the sure *guarantee* of the final glory. It is impossible to understand Paul's emphasis on the experienced life of the Spirit apart from this eschatological perspective that dominates his thinking.

> *Pivotal to the Spirit's central role is the thoroughly eschatological framework within which Paul both experienced and understood the Spirit.*

4. *God Dwelling in and among Us.* Related to the critical eschatological framework are several converging facts which demonstrate that for Paul the experience of the promised Spirit meant the return of God's personal presence to dwell in and among his people. The Spirit marks off God's people individually and corporately as God's temple, the place of his personal dwelling on earth. Brought together here in terms of fulfillment are: (a) the theme of the presence of God, expressed in the Old Testament tabernacle and temple; (b) the presence further understood in terms of the

Spirit of the Lord (Isa 63:9-14; Ps 106:33); and (c) the promised new covenant of the Spirit from Jeremiah and Ezekiel, wherein the Spirit would indwell God's people and cause them to live and to follow in his ways.

For Paul the experience of the promised Spirit meant the return of God's personal presence to dwell in and among his people.

Paul not only sees these themes as fulfilled by the gift of the Spirit, but also understands the Spirit as God's personal presence. This understanding best accounts for Paul's general reluctance to refer to the Spirit with impersonal images; on the contrary, he regularly refers to the Spirit's activity with verbs of personal action, used elsewhere of God and Christ. The Spirit is thus "the Holy Spirit of God" and "the Spirit of Jesus Christ"—the way God is currently present with and among his people.

5. *"God Very God."* In this vein it is also important to note how absolutely fundamental to Paul's theology are his presuppositions about the Trinity—although that is neither his language nor his major focus. What makes the Trinity foundational for him, without his ever discussing it as such, are the four ever-present realities (1) that God is one and personal, (2) that the Spirit is the Spirit of God and therefore personal, (3) that the Spirit and Christ are fully divine, and (4) that the Spirit is as distinct from Christ and the Father as they are from each other. This modification of Paul's understanding of the one God is in part what makes his treatment of salvation dynamic and effective.

6. *Salvation Made Effective.* Paul's understanding of God as Trinity, including the role of the Spirit, is thus foundational to the primary passion of his life—salvation in Christ. Salvation is God's activity, from beginning to end: God the Father initiated it, in that it belongs to God's eternal purposes (1 Cor 2:6-9), it has its origins in God and has God as its ultimate goal (1 Cor 8:6), and it was set in motion by God's having sent both the Son and the Spirit (Gal 4:4-7). Christ the Son accomplished salvation for the people of God through his death and resurrection, the central

feature of all of Paul's theology. The effective application in believers' lives of the love of God as offered by the Son is uniquely the work of the Spirit.

So much is this so that when Paul reminds believers of their conversion experience or of their present status in Christ, he almost always does so in terms of the Spirit's activity or presence. There is no salvation in Christ that is not fully trinitarian in this sense, and therefore there is no salvation in Christ that is not made effective in the life of the believer by the experienced coming of the Spirit, whom God "poured out on us generously through Jesus Christ our Savior" (Titus 3:6 NIV).

7. A People Called Forth. The goal of God's eschatological salvation is to create a people for his name. This people are the true succession of the old covenant people of God, and as a people are the object of God's saving activity in Christ. But they are now newly constituted through the death and resurrection of Christ and the gift of the eschatological Spirit, though they enter the community individually through faith in Christ and the gift of the Spirit.

The Spirit is thus the empowering presence of God for living the life of God in the present.

Formed by the Spirit, they are an eschatological people, who live the life of the future in the present as they await the consummation. They are God's family, evidenced by the Spirit's crying *Abba* from within their hearts; they are God's temple, the place of his habitation on earth by his Spirit; and they form Christ's body, made so by their common lavish experience of the one Spirit.

8. Righteousness Made Possible. The Spirit's major role in Paul's view lies with his being the essential element of the whole of Christian life, from beginning to end. The Spirit thus empowers ethical life in all its dimensions—individually, within the community, and to the world. Believers in Christ, who are Spirit people first and foremost, are variously described as living by the Spirit, walking in the Spirit, being led by the Spirit, bearing the fruit of the Spirit, and sowing to the Spirit. Ethics for Paul is likewise founded in the Trinity: the Spirit of God conforms the believer into the likeness of Christ to the glory of God. The Spirit is thus the empowering presence of God for living the life of God in the present.

There is therefore no Christian life that is not at the same time a *holy* life, made so by the Holy Spirit whom God gives to his people (1 Thess 4:8). At the same time, life in the Spirit also includes every other imaginable dimension of the believer's present end-time existence, including being empowered by the Spirit to abound in hope, to live in joy, to pray without ceasing, to exercise self-control, to experience a robust conscience, to have insight into God's will and purposes, and to endure in every kind of present hardship and suffering. To be a believer means nothing less than being filled with and thus to live in and by the Spirit.

9. *The Key to Christian Worship.* Finally, the Spirit is the key to all truly Christian Spirituality. At the individual level the life of the Spirit includes "praying in the Spirit" as well as with the mind. In so doing, the Spirit not only helps believers by interceding for them in their weaknesses, but also gives them great confidence in such times of prayer since God knows the mind of the Spirit, and since the Spirit prays through the believer in keeping with God's own purposes.

At the same time, the Spirit's presence, including his *charismata,* helps to build up the believing community as its members gather together to worship God. In Paul's churches, therefore, worship is "charismatic" simply because the Spirit is the key player in all that transpires. The Spirit, who forms the body and creates the temple, is present with unity and diversity, so that all may participate and all may be built up.

THE SPIRIT IN THE LATER CHURCH: A CONTRAST

With no intent to be judgmental, I observe that in much of its subsequent history the church has lived somewhat below the picture of the life of the Spirit just outlined. Indeed, the general marginalizing of the Spirit by scholarship and the frequent domestication of the Spirit by the church were noted in the overture as part of the reason for this book. For example, the passage of time and the (necessary, but not always helpful) institutionalizing of the church, plus the influence of Greek thought forms on its theologizing, led the church away from its fundamentally eschatological outlook (point 3 above). This meant the experience of the Spirit played a less and less crucial role in the church's understanding of itself as living between the times—that is, between the beginning of the end and its consummation at the return of Christ (point 7). As a result, the local community of believers was less apt to maintain the balance of being in the world but not of the world, always calling it into question, not conditioned by its values and lifestyle.

At the same time, the dynamic and experienced nature of life in the Spirit was generally lost (point 2). At least part of the reason for this was the result of a matter the New Testament never addresses: How do children of believers become believers themselves? At some point in time the majority of Christians became so as the result of being born into Christian homes rather than through adult conversion. Indeed, much of the tension later believers feel between their own experience of church and that about which they read in the New Testament can be attributed to this significant factor.

An important point is that all of Paul's letters were written to first-generation believers, all of whom—at least those *addressed* in Paul's letters—were adult converts, whose conversions had included an experience of the Holy Spirit coming into their lives. That, at least, is the picture that emerges in the letters. But what happens to this experienced conversion, attended by the Spirit, for children born and raised in the homes of such converts? As much as anything, this probably accounts for the subsequent loss of the experiential nature of life in the Spirit and for the general marginalizing of the Spirit in the later church.

Again, this is not intended to be a judgmental picture, nor do I suggest that it is true at all times and in all places. But it is of some interest that the subsequent study of church history by the church itself has far more often been a history of the institution than of the life of the Spirit in the community of faith as it lived out the life of Christ in the world.

What was not lost in all this, of course, was the *doctrine* of the Spirit, with its properly biblical understanding of the Spirit in personal terms (point 4), which led to the more formal expressions, in the creeds, of the Spirit's place in the Godhead (point 5) and therefore of his essential role in one's becoming a child of God (point 6). Related to this development are two other matters: associating the reception of the Spirit with water baptism, and the (probably) eventual practice of baptizing infant children born into Christian homes. The Spirit was inevitably now no longer perceived as dynamically experienced (point 2), although he was still a central factor in the *theology* of salvation.

The general loss of the dynamic and experiential life of the Spirit on entrance to Christian life (conversion) also accounts for the spiritual dis-ease and feebleness in the individual believer throughout much of the church's later history (point 8). This is not true of everyone, of course. But it does in part account for the rise both of the monastic movement and of various Spirit movements throughout church history. "Holy" and its plural noun, "the saints," which in Paul's Spirituality describe everyday Christian life and Christians, respectively, came to describe the special rather than the normal. So too with Spirituality (point 9). Spontaneity by the many gave way to performance by a few; prayer in the Spirit became fixed in the (often excellent) liturgy of the church; tongues did indeed generally cease and the prophetic word was relegated to the prepared sermon.

Paul's perspective of life in the Spirit, as a dynamically experienced reality creating an end-time people who live for God's glory, has not generally fared well in the overall life of the church.

To be sure, the church has also had its history of Spirit movements of various and sundry kinds. Some of these were absorbed into the church; others were pushed outside the church and usually became heretical and divisive; and still others became reform movements within the church. The common denominator of most of these movements has been their attempt to recapture the life of the Spirit in some form. To the degree that they succeeded they have been a source of renewal and blessing. But Spirit movements tend to make institutions nervous—for good reason, one might add, both positively and negatively. The net result has been that Paul's perspective of life in the Spirit, as a dynamically experienced reality creating an end-time people who live for God's glory, has not generally fared well in the overall life of the church.

A WAY FORWARD

If what has preceded paints too bleak a picture or sounds like a belittling of the subsequent work of the Spirit in the church, let me say again that this is not my intent; nor do I think that if we could turn the clock back, all would be better. To the contrary, I not only recognize that the clock cannot be turned back, but also find cause for much rejoicing in the church's history. The creeds, the liturgies, the theologizing, the institutional life are not only with us, but for many, myself included, are seen to be the work of the Spirit in the subsequent life of the church. The plea of this study, therefore, is not that of a restorationist, as if we really could restore "the primitive church," whatever that means and whatever that would look like. Rather, it is a plea for recapturing Paul's perspective of Christian life as essentially the life of the Spirit, dynamically experienced and eschatologically oriented—but fully integrated into the life of the church.

From my limited perspective, such a recapturing has three dimensions. First, we need the Spirit to bring life into our present institutions, theologies, and liturgies—in contrast to tearing down these barns and building different ones, which all too often has been the history of Spirit movements, especially of the restorationist type. The Spirit not only inspires a new body of songs in every renewal within the church, but makes the best of former hymns come to life with new vigor. "Can these dry bones live?" the Lord asked the prophet. "You know," he replied, and then watched as the Spirit brought life to what was already there. Too much water has passed under the bridge for us to believe that somehow we will be miraculously unified in terms of visible structures, liturgies, and theologies. But time and again, when the human factor is not getting in the way, the Spirit has given God's people a greater sense that they are one across confessional lines. The church is with us—indeed, we are it—in its present shape(s) and structures. May the Spirit of the living God be poured out upon us afresh for our life in the present world until Christ comes again.

Second, a genuine recapturing of Paul's perspective will not isolate the Spirit in such a way that Spiritual gifts and Spirit phenomena take pride of place in the church, resulting in churches that are either charismatic or otherwise. Rather, a genuine recapturing of Paul's perspective will cause the church to be more vitally trinitarian, not only in its theology but in its life and Spirituality as well. This will mean not the exaltation of the Spirit but the exaltation of God; and it will mean focus not on the Spirit as such but on the Son, crucified and risen, Savior and Lord of all. Ethical life will be neither narrowly, individualistically imagined nor legalistically expressed, but will be joyously communal and decidedly over against the world's present trinity of relativism, secularism, and individualism, with their thoroughly dehumanizing results. And the proper trinitarian aim of such ethics will be Paul's own aim—to the glory of God, through being conformed to the image of the Son, by the empowering of the Spirit.

Recapturing the dynamic life of the Spirit will also entail the renewal of the *charismata*, not for the sake of being charismatic, but for the building up of the people of God for their life together and in the world. What must not happen in such a renewal is what has so often happened in the past: holding the extraordinary *charismata* in such awe that they are allowed to exist untested, undiscerned, and ungrounded in the local body of believers. Every form of extremism, which is often the expressed or hidden fear over a renewed life of the Spirit in the church, is ultimately the result of failure to heed Paul's key injunction (1 Thess 5:19–22):

"Do not quench the Spirit by despising prophesying. But *test all things*; and in so doing, hold fast to what is good and be done with every evil form." The failure to test the spirits has led to lack of responsibility and accountability, which in turn has often led to failure on the part of some who were in prominence, as well as to pain and hurt by those who were the recipients of prophetic words that were either false or impossible.

Third, a genuine recapturing of the dynamic life of the Spirit will result in more effective evangelism in a lost, isolated, individualistic world. As evidenced already in some good ways through current charismatic traditions and traditional Pentecostals, the visibly dynamic work of the Spirit—where God is less an item in the creed and more obviously at work in the world—has frequently manifested itself in drawing people to Christ and into his church. Our task is not to share our "good views" about God, but to offer his great and glorious "good news," which includes his presence as reality in people's lives and in the life of the church.

In summary, I think Paul's perspective has the better of it; and I also believe that that perspective can become our own—dare I say, must become our own, if we are going to make any difference at all in the so-called post-Christian, postmodern era. But this means that our theologizing must stop paying mere lip service to the Spirit and recognize his crucial role in Paul's gospel; and it means that the church must risk freeing the Spirit from being boxed into the creed and getting him back into the experiential life of the believer and the believing community.

—

So we have come to the end of this look at the Spirit in Paul's letters. What is obviously missing is the how to question, which is probably the more urgent question for most people in a culture like ours. "How do I foster such a life of the Spirit within my church?" and "What do I do personally about all of this?" are the most frequently asked questions in seminars when I present this material.

On the corporate level my response is basically to the leadership, for without the leadership taking ownership of the need, little will happen. To leaders, then, I suggest three things: First, over a long period teach this material in an ongoing way. Teach the people biblically. Work hard on the texts themselves. Lead the people through Paul's letters again and again, pointing out the crucial role the Spirit plays in his view of things.

Second, I refer back to the first paragraphs of chapter 5. I would make it my top priority to lead the people of God into a more biblical understanding of what it means for us to be God's eschatological *people* in a world gone mad. Over and over again, through text after text, New Testament book after New Testament book, I would try to help them to make a major paradigm shift as to what it means to be the people of God in the world. Since this is the aim of God's saving work in Christ that the Spirit has come to bring to realization, I would make this the focus of ministry for years to come.

"Seek earnestly the better gifts" for the edification of the body is an imperative, not a polite invitation.

Third, in terms of the gathered community at worship (chs. 13 and 14 above), leaders would do well to provide a setting and atmosphere in which people can practice. This means readiness to take risks by creating opportunities in a corporate setting to let the *charismata* build up the people of God—for growth in ministry within and in reaching out to the world. Take risks as leaders and then be willing to get out of the way to let the people of God function as a whole priesthood, each one bringing their gifts to God and to each other. Allow for newness, changes, and greater spontaneity within the structures God has traditionally blessed. After all, "seek earnestly the better gifts" for the edification of the body is an imperative, not a polite invitation.

At the individual level, my stock answer is admittedly not always helpful: hunger and thirst with openness. For some this puts too much emphasis on the human rather than on the divine side; and I too fear that. But my own experience in the church is that there is a clear correlation between our own hunger after God, on the one hand, and our experience of God, on the other. This does not remove the experience of the Spirit from God's own sovereignty, nor does it imply that the one hungering and thirsting does not already have the Spirit in full measure. I simply know of no other practical solution.

Moreover, our Lord himself pronounced his congratulatory blessing on those who "hunger and thirst after righteousness," promising that they "shall be filled." Part of the point of this book is that hungering and thirsting after the life of the Spirit is what that beatitude is all about. And that beatitude presupposes the first one, that those who recognize themselves before God as "impoverished in spirit [S/spirit?]" are the inheritors of the kingdom.

The concern for openness is where I would emphasize the divine sovereignty. It is a way of suggesting that we need less often to tell God what we want, as though we knew what is best for us, and more often to have a stance of openness, so that we might continually be surprised by joy. Openness means seeking earnestly after the Spirit, with readiness for whatever the Spirit may want to do, not for the sake of our individual walk alone, but for what it will mean for sake of the body. My experience over many years, including the reading of Scripture, has taught me that the one God, who lives in holy joy and love in triune relationship, delights to delight his people, and those delights are as diverse as the creation itself.

Perhaps the proper way to conclude this study, therefore, is with prayer, in this case with the aid of earlier Spirit-inspired prayers. The first is from Psalms, expressing the longing of those who already know God to know him more—and better; it assumes the attitude of the first and fourth beatitudes, but is expressed in the passionate language of the soul that knows it has a God-shaped space within, which desperately needs God to fill it with himself:

> O God, you are my God,
>   earnestly I seek you;
> my soul thirsts for you,
>   my body longs for you,
> in a dry and weary land
>   where there is no water. (63:1 NIV)

The second is the prayer of Moses, noted earlier as lying close to the surface of Paul's understanding of the Spirit as God's empowering presence. Here is that cry of desperation which should mark church and believer alike, who live as God's redeemed and redemptive people in the postmodern era that marks the turning of the centuries—and millennia:

> If your Presence does not go with us, do not send us up from here. How will anyone know that you are pleased with . . . your people unless you go with us? What else will distinguish . . . your people from all the other people on the face of the earth? (Exod 33:15–16 NIV)

Finally, from Andrew Reed's hymn, which expresses at the individual level what should perhaps most characterize the nature of our prayer for life in the Spirit:

> Holy Spirit, all divine,
> Dwell within this heart of mine;
> Cast down every idol throne,
> Reign supreme, and reign alone.

Amen and amen.

SPIRIT BAPTISM AND WATER BAPTISM IN PAUL

I began writing the material in this appendix as a chapter of its own, between those on "getting in" and "staying in." But from the outset I had some difficulties with it—partly because I feared that by interrupting the flow of the material in chapters 7 through 10, it might also deflect from my primary concerns in this book. The light dawned when I suddenly realized that it was the only chapter in the book in which the questions raised did not emerge from our reading of Paul himself, but by our coming to Paul with later agendas in hand. That realization caught my attention, and in itself should tell us something. Thus I offer my observations on Paul's stance on these questions in an appendix.

In some ways, these issues present a no-win situation, since most Christians have vested interests on either side and tend to come to the biblical texts with their convictions in hand. Here in particular the issue is clouded by the fact that in a mere thirteen letters, we do not have everything Paul ever thought or said on a lot of questions, especially on this sticky one. But we do have some data, so let's see where it leads us.

At issue are two matters arising from chapter 8 above.[1] On the one side is the question of baptism. At issue is the relationship between baptism in water and the experience of the Spirit. Some see that relationship to be close, in that the Spirit is understood to be received at baptism. For others, there is no relationship at all, unless it is coincidental. We might use the narratives of Acts to help us focus the question: Is the paradigm the story in Acts 19:1–7, where the coming of the Spirit happens in conjunction with baptism, or is it the story in Acts 10, where baptism is in response to the prior coming of the Spirit?

On the other side is the question of the more dynamic, experiential evidence of the Spirit's coming, which we noted in chapter 8 was part of the bigger picture of what happens to a person at the entry point of salvation in Christ. A substantial tradition in the church believes that such an experience of the Spirit, a "baptism in the Spirit" if you will, is available to believers *subsequent* to their reception of the Spirit in conversion—although the purpose of the subsequent Spirit baptism has been variously understood (sanctification, empowering, confirmation). Here the narrative in Acts 8 serves as the paradigm (conversion, followed by baptism, followed at a later time by Spirit baptism).

These issues are much larger than we can deal with here, because in this case the rest of the New Testament witness is especially important. My interest in this book is strictly with the Pauline witness; and since he has so little to say about the second question, that of Spirit baptism, I will expand my purview to see whether the Pauline evidence might be amenable to the concept of "subsequence."

The data can be easily put forth. Paul associates the Spirit with the verb "to baptize" in a single text, 1 Corinthians 12:13; and on this text a lot has been written—with a great deal of disagreement.[2] Since this passage has been used by all sides to support their positions, I here offer a somewhat detailed analysis, with these two questions in mind.

THE SPIRIT AND WATER BAPTISM

In the early church water baptism was the believer's immediate response to God's saving action by the Spirit. Since some of the texts discussed in chapter 8 seem to some to suggest a close connection between the two, they have argued that the Spirit actually comes to the believer through the event of baptism itself—much like the dove descended on Jesus in the waters of baptism, which is viewed as a model for later Christians.[3] The key texts here are 1 Corinthians 6:11; 12:13; and Titus 3:5, although some would add Galatians 3:28–4:6 and the imagery of the seal in 2 Corinthians 1:21–22; Ephesians 1:13–14; and 4:30.[4]

The problem here is partly one of method (how does one proceed to discover Paul's perspective?) and partly one of traditional presuppositions (one tends to argue on the basis of one's own experience of the church, not on the basis of the biblical evidence as a whole).[5] There are basically three avenues of approach, none of which is totally free of bias: (1) to look carefully at texts that actually—or seem to—associate water baptism and the Spirit; (2) to look at texts where Paul speaks about water baptism in a clear, unambiguous way, and see whether they might also connect to the Spirit in some way; and (3) to look at the texts where conversion is clearly expressed in terms of the Spirit and see whether baptism might also be presupposed.

"Baptism in the Spirit" in 1 Corinthians 12:13

In 1 Corinthians 12:13, following the twofold assertion that "the body is one" and that it "is made up of many parts," Paul goes on to explain the first assertion by saying, "for indeed we all were baptized in one Spirit so as to form one body—whether Jews or Greek, slave or free—and we were all given one Spirit to drink to the fill." Some see the language "baptized in one Spirit" as evidence that Paul saw the gifting of the Spirit to be intimately related to water baptism; others see the second clause, "all given one Spirit to drink," as evidence for a work of the Spirit subsequent to the first one. Both points of view run aground when the passage is looked at closely in its context.[6]

The context is one in which Paul and the Corinthians are at odds over what constitutes true "Spirituality." The Corinthians apparently see glossolalia (speaking in tongues) as evidence that they have already begun to speak the language of heaven (13:1), indicating that they have already arrived in a spiritual state that more or less puts them above life in the present world. This understanding of the Spirit appears to lie behind most of the ills in this letter. Paul has a different view of Spirituality, which includes discipleship that follows the Crucified One (see 2:1-3; 4:8-9; etc.).

To straighten out their view on glossolalia he chooses to argue first theologically, which he does in chapter 12, that their singular focus on speaking in tongues misunderstands, and therefore misrepresents, the nature of the church. The Corinthians are deeply divided on some other matters, but apparently promote (or at least some do) uniformity when it comes to the Spirit's manifestations; Paul urges diversity within unity as the true evidence of the Spirit's presence among them, which is the point of almost the whole of chapter 12. But in v. 13, in elaboration of his first assertion in v. 12, he offers the ground of their unity, namely, their common lavish experience of the Spirit.

Paul's concern in this sentence, therefore, is not to delineate how an individual becomes a believer (the question most people come to the text with), but to explain how the many of them, diverse as they are, are in fact one body. The answer: The Spirit, whom all alike have received.

To make that point Paul refers to their common reception of the Spirit, presumably at the beginning of their Christian experience, by means of parallel clauses:

We all were baptized in the one Spirit,

and

We all were caused to drink one Spirit.

The first clause is further qualified by the prepositional phrase (in Greek), "so as to become one body," which in turn is modified by the parenthetical addition, "whether Jews or Greeks, slave or free." Several important observations follow from this analysis.

1. While some argue that Paul's use of the verb "baptized" must refer to the rite of Christian initiation, that is not at all certain. It is true that early on this verb became the technical term for that rite; but one may not thereby assume that Paul intended its technical sense here. He does not say "we were all *baptized*," which on its own would almost certainly imply "with water"; rather, he says specifically, "we were all *baptized in the Spirit.*"

2. Moreover, it is clearly not baptism but the *one* Spirit, repeated in both clauses, that in Paul's present argument is the basis for unity (cf. vv. 4–11). This is Paul's consistent perspective throughout his letters: believers form one body in Christ precisely because of the "one Spirit."

3. The text does not support the view that the Spirit is received at water baptism. The Greek preposition *en* ("in/with/by") can hardly be stretched to mean something like, "we were all baptized (in water) and thereby given the Spirit." Here the Spirit is either the element into which they have all been baptized (as I think), or the agent by which they have been baptized to become one body.

4. The greater difficulty for the view that the Spirit is received at water baptism lies with the second clause, "and we were all given one Spirit to drink to the fill." This is most likely an instance of Semitic parallelism, where both clauses make essentially the same point. It is the clearly metaphorical sense of this parallel clause that, along with the modifier "in the Spirit," argues most strongly for a metaphorical, rather than literal, meaning for "baptism" in the first clause. That is, their experience of the Spirit is analogous to, but not identical with, their immersion in water at baptism. They were immersed in the Spirit.

5. Some—on all sides, interestingly enough—have argued that the second clause points to a *second* (definite, recognizable) experience in the Spirit. But against such a view is the parallelism just noted, plus the lack of such language elsewhere in the whole of Christian literature to refer to an experience of the Spirit.

In light of these observations, to what may we presume the two clauses to refer? For what Christian experience do they serve as metaphors? Some have argued for Spirit baptism, by which they mean a separate and distinguishable experience from conversion. But this has against it both Pauline usage (he does not elsewhere use this term or clearly point to such a second experience) and the emphasis in this context, which is not on a special experience in the Spirit beyond conversion, but on their *common* reception of the Spirit.

Most likely, therefore, Paul is referring to their common experience of conversion, and he does so in terms of its most crucial ingredient, the receiving of the Spirit. Such expressive metaphors (immersion in the Spirit and drinking to the fill of the Spirit) imply a much greater experiential and visibly manifest reception of the Spirit than many have tended to experience in subsequent church history. Paul can make such an appeal to their common experience of the Spirit as the presupposition for the unity of the body precisely because, as in Galatians 3:2-5, the Spirit was a dynamically experienced reality, which had happened to all (cf. chapter 8 above).

The goal of their common immersion in the one Spirit is "into/ unto one body," which of course is the point in context, picking up the concern of v. 12. Indeed, this phrase expresses the reason for the sentence in the first place. How did the many of them, diverse as they are, all become one body? By their common, lavish experience of one and the same Spirit.

To emphasize that the many ("we all") have become one through the Spirit, Paul adds parenthetically, "whether Jews or Greeks, slave or free." These terms express the two basic distinctions that separated people in that culture—race (in Judaism synonymous with religion) and social status. In Christ these old distinctions have been obliterated, not in the sense that one is no longer Jew or Greek, and so on, but in the sense of their having significance. Having significance is what gives them value as distinctives. So in effect their common experience of the Spirit had eliminated the significance of the old distinctions, hence they had become one body.

That, at least, is Paul's concern. It is therefore unlikely that, even though the lavish quality of the metaphor finds its meaning in their immersion in water, Paul is connecting the Spirit with that rite. It is equally unlikely that he intends to refer to a second experience beyond conversion called Spirit baptism either by this language or by adding the second metaphor of "drinking to the fill."

Other Passages Alleged to Associate Water Baptism and the Spirit

Some of the same problems exist with 1 Corinthians 6:11 and Titus 3:5 as with 1 Corinthians 12:13. But in these cases, the language of baptism is missing altogether. As pointed out in the discussion of these passages in chapter 8 above, the metaphor "washing" may well allude to the waters of baptism. But in neither case is Paul suggesting that the Spirit is received at baptism.

Indeed, it is quite otherwise. Not only does he intend to say in 1 Corinthians 6:11 that they have been "washed" from their defilement of sin, but they have been so washed by the twin agency of Christ and the Spirit. The Spirit as the agent of the cleansing from sin scarcely implies that he is received at baptism. The same holds true for Titus 3:6–7. We also noted in chapter 8 that it is altogether unlikely that Paul understood the image "seal" to refer to baptism—especially so, since in one of these passages at least the seal is equated with the Spirit (2 Cor 1:21–22, "God sealed you by giving you the Holy Spirit"), not baptism.

The only connection between baptism and the Spirit in any these passages is coincidental, that is, the images for baptism and the mention of the Spirit happen to occur in the same sentence. What is missing is a direct link between the rite of baptism as such and the coming of the Spirit. In no place does Paul express the kind of relationship between the two that those assume who assert that at baptism one *receives* the Spirit. In most of these passages, apart from those referring to the Spirit as the seal of redemption, the Spirit is the agent of the immersion or washing. That Paul understood one to receive the Spirit through the waters of baptism would require at least one piece of explicit evidence.

Explicit References to Water Baptism

Paul's explicit references to water baptism further indicate a lack of direct relationship with the gift of the Spirit: 1 Corinthians 1:13–17 (cf. 10:2; 15:29); Galatians 3:27; Romans 6:3–4; Colossians 2:12; Ephesians 4:5. Two features about these passages stand out. First, in every instance the association between the believer and baptism is invariably with reference to Christ, not to the Spirit. Two instances are especially instructive. In Galatians 3:27 Paul refers to "putting on Christ." This kind of language is strikingly missing throughout his writings with regard to the Spirit. That is, in baptism one is pictured as being clothed with Christ, but never so with the Spirit. Moreover, in Ephesians 4:4–6 Paul deliberately, in a creedlike way, associates various aspects of Christian life with the Spirit and with Christ. The one body and one hope are associated with the Spirit; faith and baptism are associated with Christ.

Second, in 1 Corinthians 1:13–17 Paul deliberately portrays baptism as secondary to the proclamation of the gospel. This does not mean that he minimizes baptism; but he will not allow that it holds the same level of significance as the preaching of Christ that brought people to faith. My point: in this same argument he specifically associates the receiving of the Spirit with his proclaiming of the gospel, not with baptism. In Paul's mind baptism stands on a different level, apparently as a response of the believer to the grace received through the Spirit upon accepting the proclaimed word in faith.

One is hard-pressed to imagine that Paul could speak so casually of baptism and of his having baptized only two of them (plus one household that he had to be reminded of!), if he had understood the Spirit to come at their baptism. But in 1 Corinthians 2:1–5, he insists that the Spirit came on them precisely at the point of his ministry, through his proclaiming of the word. This would hardly be true if the Spirit came during baptism, since Paul baptized so few of them.

This last text seems conclusive that Paul understood the Spirit as being received at conversion, in the hearing of the gospel by faith, not later at baptism. This is not to say that at times what Luke pictures in a passage like Acts 19:1–7 did not happen in the Pauline context. But what all of this evidence together does suggest is that the close tie of water baptism to the Spirit does not come from a close reading of Paul, but stems from reading back into Paul the later experience of the church.

CONVERSION AND SPIRIT BAPTISM

The urgent question on the other side is whether Paul also conceived of a work of grace beyond conversion to which the language "the baptism of the Spirit" might correctly apply. Although some of Paul's texts have been interpreted in this way (e.g., 1 Cor 12:13; Gal 4:4–6),[7] the full evidence of these passages in context makes this doubtful. Whether Paul knew of such an experience is a moot point, argued against primarily on the basis of silence. Two further points need to be made.

First, Paul makes a clear connection between the Spirit and the experience of power. What becomes evident from the discussion in chapter 8 above is that the Spirit was not merely experienced in conversion but experienced in a dynamic, undoubtedly visible, way. This is precisely why Paul appeals to the lavish experience of the Spirit to make his points in both Galatians 3:2–4 and 1 Corinthians 12:13. This is made the more certain by Galatians 3:5, where as further evidence that the Galatians have no relationship to the Jewish law, Paul appeals specifically to their ongoing experience of the Spirit as dynamically present among them with miraculous deeds—one can scarcely interpret the two present tenses otherwise ("God gives the Spirit and works miracles among you"). By reemphasizing this dimension of Christian life in their experience of "baptism," Spirit movements tend (correctly, I would argue) to think they have recaptured an experience at the heart of Paul's understanding of the Spirit and Christian life, even if they have (less convincingly) also made a virtue out of their timing of this dimension as well.[8]

Second, Paul does not see life in the Spirit as the result of a single experience of the Spirit at the entry point. He simply did not have the static view of the Spirit that so many later Christians seem to have—that the Spirit is "given" once for all at conversion, and after that we are pretty much left to our own devices to live out the Christian life. For Paul the Spirit is the key to all of Christian life, and he implies frequently there are further, ongoing times of receiving the Spirit's empowering.

This point is certainly intended in Galatians 3:5; it is the further implication of such present tense verbs as in 1 Thessalonians 4:8 and Ephesians 5:18, and the consequence of prayer in Philippians 1:19. In 1 Thessalonians 4:8 Paul's first reference is surely to their conversion; but the argument in context and the verb's present tense ("God *gives* you his Holy Spirit") imply that what happened at conversion needs to be renewed in light of their pagan past. All of this suggests that perhaps too much is made on both sides of single experiences.

For Paul life in the Spirit begins at conversion; at the same time its experienced dimension is both dynamic and renewable. Water baptism is the believer's response to the Spirit's prior presence and activity. The Pauline images for baptism, death and resurrection and "being clothed with Christ," suggest that it is not merely a rite. It is part and parcel of the whole conversion complex. Because immersion was the normal mode of baptism, it provided Paul with rich metaphors to indicate the role of baptism in the complex. Through baptism believers reenact their association with Christ at its deepest level; they have "died" and are "buried" with him, and in him they "rise from death" to walk in newness of life. Thus they "put on Christ." But for Paul the key to both our being given life and our walking in newness of life is the Spirit.

Moreover, the reception of the Spirit is not a static or merely past event, but is pictured as an ongoing reality. Quantitative language is strictly avoided; that is, one does not get more or get filled again. Nonetheless, the experience of the ever-present Spirit can be fanned into flame. At issue should not be terminology or theological fine tuning, but constant renewing so that we might be truly people of the Spirit in our present world.

NOTES

1. For the most substantial treatment of these two questions, covering the whole range of the New Testament, see J. D. G. Dunn, *Baptism in the Holy Spirit* (London: SCM, 1970). He was responded to in detail from the charismatic side by H. V. Ervin, *Conversion-Initiation and the Baptism of the Holy Spirit* (Peabody, Mass.: Hendrickson, 1984); but Ervin's exegesis is often forced, marring the overall value of the book.

2. There is also considerable disagreement even on the terminology, since many, on the basis of 1 Cor 12:13, are prone to use the term "Spirit baptism" to refer to conversion itself.

3. A model, interestingly, that Pentecostals have seen as expressing Spirit baptism as subsequent to his birth by the Spirit.

4. What follows is based on the analysis of these texts from *GEP*.

5. One reads in Hoyle (*Holy Spirit,* 32), for example, that "in the early church . . . the reception of the Spirit *generally followed* upon baptism, though in exceptional cases it might precede it" (emphasis mine), with the "exceptions" in Acts noted in a footnote. Since the "exceptions" are significantly more numerous than the "rule," one might think that in this case the exception was the rule!

6. For a more detailed presentation of this perspective, see *GEP,* 82–84, or the introduction to my commentary on 1 Corinthians.

7. See, e.g., Horton, *What the Bible Says about the Holy Spirit,* 215–17; cf. 173. So also Ervin, *Conversion-Initiation,* 98–102, 86–88, and H. Hunter, *Spirit-Baptism: A Pentecostal Alternative* (Lanham, Md.: University Press of America, 1983). Pages 39–42, 35–36.

8. On this question, see G. D. Fee, "Baptism in the Holy Spirit: The Issue of Separability and Subsequence," in *Gospel and Spirit* (Peabody, Mass.: Hendrickson, 1991) 105–19.

SCRIPTURE INDEX